"*Building the Body* powerfully draws on the biblical imagery of the church while taking the concept of church health to a whole new level. Becoming fit is presented in a way that motivates rather than produces guilt, and the combination of principles and practices apply to churches at all levels of development. A practical resource to read individually or share with a group that will remain a valuable reference long after it is first read."

—Wayne Schmidt, general superintendent,
the Wesleyan Church

"Have you ever said, 'I can get in shape if I want to'? Do you do anything about it? *Building the Body* is a practical, informative, doable resource for leaders and churches who want not only to get better but also to get as strong or fit as possible for the good of the kingdom of Jesus Christ. . . . Keep this one handy in your everyday ministry and leadership regimen!"

—Dr. Jim Dunn, vice president of church relations,
Wesleyan Investment Foundation

"Fitness of any kind is a matter of knowing what to do and committing to it. You may be really committed to do something but wind up doing all the wrong things or you may know a lot but have no will to do it. In *Building the Body*, using physical fitness as an analogy, Gary and Phil bring will and knowledge into helpful focus. You will be motivated and informed to higher levels of effectiveness in your church. And while physical fitness is a good way to add a few years to your stay on earth, church fitness opens eternity to a lot of other people!"

—Rev. Kevin Mannoia, chaplain, Azusa Pacific University;
president of the International Council for Higher Education;
founder and chair, Wesleyan Holiness Connection

"Practical steps to the next level—that's what this book offers. Wherever your church lies along a continuum of twelve factors (e.g., outreach, stewardship, worship, disciple making), McIntosh and Stevenson give concrete strategies for advancing to the next level . . . and then the next level . . . and then the next level."

—Donald R. Sunukjian, chair, Department of Christian Ministry and Leadership, Talbot School of Theology

"Your church might be healthy but not fit. Gary McIntosh and Phil Stevenson are two outstanding church leaders who have once again delivered an insightful book that will help pastors and volunteer leaders develop a church this is truly 'fit.' I think the practical genius of the book is found in the specific applications that are organized into five categories of churches: beginner, novice, intermediate, advanced, and elite. Identify which church you are and dig in!"

—Dan Reiland, executive pastor, 12Stone Church

"*Building the Body* is full of practical, next-step ideas for churches that want to be 'fit' to effectively join Jesus on the mission field and impact their communities. Gary and Phil, pulling from their years of experience working with churches and church leaders, provide tools to help understand your starting point and how to adjust priorities and identify action items to move toward being 'fit' for the mission. In the church consulting world, where so much of the material is theory-based, *Building the Body* is a practical, hands-on, and helpful book."

—Lonnie J. Bullock, executive director, New Church Specialties

BUILDING
THE
BODY

BUILDING THE BODY

12 Characteristics of a **FIT CHURCH**

GARY L. MCINTOSH
AND PHIL STEVENSON

BakerBooks

a division of Baker Publishing Group
Grand Rapids, Michigan

Published by Baker Books
a division of Baker Publishing Group
PO Box 6287, Grand Rapids, MI 49516-6287
www.bakerbooks.com

Printed in the United States of America

Library of Congress Cataloging-in-Publication Data
Names: McIntosh, Gary, 1947– author.
Title: Building the body : 12 characteristics of a fit church / Gary L. McIntosh and
    Phil Stevenson.
Description: Grand Rapids : Baker Books, 2018. | Includes bibliographical
    references.
Identifiers: LCCN 2017028468 | ISBN 9780801019623 (pbk.)
Subjects: LCSH: Church.
Classification: LCC BV600.3 .M3534 2018 | DDC 250—dc23
LC record available at https://lccn.loc.gov/2017028468

18 19 20 21 22 23 24   7 6 5 4 3 2 1

To my wife, Joni, who is always a source
of constant encouragement.

I am grateful to the pastoral leaders
in the Pacific-Southwest Movement
I am privileged to work with.
You men and women continually
challenge and stretch me.

—Phil Stevenson

Contents

Contents

Introduction

The Fitness Factor

Something had to change. I (Phil) could not stand to look at myself in a mirror or view myself in a picture. My face was full (a nice way of saying fat). My pant size was huge. Yet, by most indicators, I was healthy. The standard markers of health were all within range. Blood pressure? Fine. Cholesterol? Under 200. Temperature? Standard. I was free of disease and had no major illnesses. Based on popular health indicators, I was healthy. But . . . I was not fit! If someone had asked me to run a mile, I could not have done it. A big gap lies between health and fitness. People often view health as meeting a minimum standard of evaluation. Meeting this standard may provide a person with a sense of well-being, but it does not tell the entire story. An individual who desires a more effective and energetic life ought to strive for fitness.

Determining if a person is healthy, let alone fit, is not an easy matter. For example, I weighed 242 pounds, which would have been just right if I stood six foot four. However, I am five foot ten. At that height, a normal, healthy weight for a male between

25 and 59, with a large frame, is between 158 and 180 pounds.[1] Clearly, I was overweight. However, that's only part of the story. To determine if a person is overweight, the bone, muscle, and fat in their body's composition must be taken into consideration. A critical measure used by medical professionals is body mass index (BMI). A BMI higher than 24.9 is considered overweight, and my BMI was 34.7, which is considered obese. BMI is only an approximate indicator to be used as a rough guide. It does, however, provide an accurate assessment of a person's fitness.

Healthy or Fit?

Fitness implies a level of activity. After assessing my personal level of fitness, I reached a point of dissatisfaction. A mentor of mine shared with me that dissatisfaction is a one-word definition for motivation. Once I became aware of, and dissatisfied with, my fitness level, I was motivated to take the necessary steps to become fit. My plan embraced three key elements: regular exercise, food portion control, and tracking my progress. After implementing these three elements consistently as part of my lifestyle, I lost more than fifty pounds, which I have kept off. Exercise was the real key, and I chose running as my primary activity.

Runners can be categorized according to five basic levels. First, beginner runners have no experience. At this stage, a person's interest in running is more philosophical. That is, they like the idea of running and the results it will bring but have yet to test their resolve in the actual activity of running.

Second, novice runners have some background in running. They can typically run between one and three miles. The pace may not be great, but they have a propensity to achieve a higher fitness level. They have much to learn in the area of pace, nutrition, and recovery, but they are actively learning.

Third, intermediate runners can run for thirty minutes at a nine-minute-per-mile pace.[2] At this level, they are making progress in both running time and pace. They demonstrate knowledge about running and the practice of actually running well.

The late running specialist Hal Higdon defined the fourth stage, advanced runner, as one who is familiar with the training necessary to increase running efficiency and has the attitude to do so.[3] Advanced runners push themselves to increased fitness. They look for others to challenge them, and they participate in a variety of running events to develop their running expertise. In addition, they look for opportunities to share their knowledge and experience to assist others in developing their own running skills.

The top, and last, category is composed of elite runners, who compete at a much higher level than others. According to *New York Times* health and science columnist Gina Kolata, "Elite distance runners have physiological traits that make them faster than the rest of us and account for the albatross between Olympic champions and the masses of fitness and recreational runners."[4] World-class runners have a particular bent for running, and they regularly put in the hard work to achieve above-average success.

Few people, of course, are world-class runners, yet almost anyone can engage in activity to increase their level of fitness. You may never run a sub-four-minute mile, but you can run a mile. You may never compete on the world stage, but you can do better on the platform God has provided for you.

A Metaphor about Running

Churches are much like people when it comes to health and fitness. Church leaders are enamored with the concept of developing healthy churches. Unfortunately, church health does not always result in making disciples (see Matt. 28:19–20). In reality, church health in and of itself does not necessarily result in fruitfulness. Just as an individual may be healthy living a sedentary lifestyle, churches are often content with a minimum level of health. Thus, they are technically healthy but not fit.

The metaphor of long-distance runners highlights the five stages in the health and fitness of churches. First, beginner churches are extremely sedentary. They have little experience with church health concepts and do not think about church fitness. Most have had declining worship attendance for a decade or longer. They may have launched new programs to increase vitality but gave up when no results appeared immediately. Beginner churches have extremely high BMIs and may be nearer to death than life.

Second, novice churches have some understanding of church health principles and have attempted to implement specific ideas to strengthen the church. Worship attendance has often plateaued, but these churches are comfortable. While their BMIs are not as high as those of beginner churches, their comfort is akin to hypertension in humans. They can live with hypertension for many years, but if left untreated, it may result in a stroke or death.

Third, intermediate churches have achieved good levels of health. They are unified, loving, and caring. Worshipers know their spiritual gifts and passions; many serve in ministry roles. Church leaders teach the Word of God with conviction. Parents raise their children in the faith. Members support missionaries and offer prayers for the salvation of souls around the world. An intermediate level is respectable, but these churches need to move on to become fit churches.

Fourth, advanced churches are extremely fit, make new disciples each year, and have started at least one or two daughter churches. They stand out from other churches due to their higher levels of people involved in prayer, Christ-exalting worship, and missional engagement in the community. Advanced churches have a clear vision and a strong passion and effectively execute their mission.

Fifth, elite churches have attained extraordinary levels of fitness. They are called the best of the best, top in their class, A1, and exceptional. As one might expect, elite churches are rare. They are unusually gifted but also have worked long and hard to achieve high levels of fruitfulness.

Fitness Components

According to FitDay, a link accessed through the American College of Sports Medicine (ACSM), fitness has five components: (1) cardiovascular endurance, (2) muscular strength, (3) muscular endurance, (4) flexibility, and (5) body composition.[5] These components are applicable to both people and churches that desire to become fit in life and in ministry. As the apostle Paul wrote, life is a race (not a sprint but a long-distance run to be more exact), so "let us run with perseverance the race marked out for us" (Heb. 12:1 NIV). Churches ought to work on their spiritual muscles so that when the time comes, the faith community will "be strong [muscular strength] in the Lord" (Eph. 6:10) and able to remain strong [muscular endurance] in the Lord. Churches must have flexibility, because at times God will ask them to do something that may stretch them or make them feel uncomfortable. In the same way a person's body needs fuel, churches as spiritual bodies need the right balance of nutrients found in God's Word. Feeding on the Word of God strengthens the composition of church bodies, allowing them to endure any challenge that comes their way.

Developing endurance requires church leaders to remain disciplined so they will be spiritually fit and eventually hear those humbling words, "Well done, good and faithful servant!" (Matt. 25:21 NIV). Fitness requires discipline. Little effort is required to sit on a couch watching television three hours a day. However, working out moderately for thirty minutes a day, five days a week takes immense discipline. Likewise, a church can maintain a low level of health with little effort, but moving toward a high level of fitness takes immense effort. Thus, the five components of fitness—cardiovascular endurance, muscular strength, muscular endurance, flexibility, and body composition can be improved through disciplined effort. Cardiovascular endurance is the body's ability to deliver oxygen to muscles while they are working.[6]

Oxygen is the lifeblood of the body, as it is for churches. So what keeps oxygen flowing to the vital organs of a church? A focus on outreach, effective evangelism, and community engagement. These activities bring new energy to a church body to keep it living and breathing.

The second component, muscular strength, is needed to overcome resistance. Muscular strength is the highest amount of effort exerted by the muscles of the body in order to overcome the most resistance in a single effort.[7] Muscular strength influences everything the body does—from getting out of bed in the morning to getting back in bed at night and everything in between. All activity demands muscular strength. Churches need muscular strength to overcome the resistance society exerts against them. They need muscular strength to serve the community, to preach the gospel, and to build up their members. Personal ministry, God-honoring stewardship, and leadership development provide muscular strength. Each of these characteristics strengthens the spiritual muscles needed for the church body to be fit.

Closely aligned with muscular strength is muscular endurance. While muscular strength deals with exertion in a single effort, muscular endurance relates to doing something repeatedly. "Muscular endurance is the ability of a muscle or group of muscles to repeatedly exert force against resistance."[8] The characteristics that provide for muscular endurance are Christ-exalting worship, disciple-making strategy, and pastoral leadership. These characteristics provide the needed strength to continue for the long haul.

12 Characteristics of a Fit Church

- Outreach
- Effective Evangelism
- Community Engagement
- Personal Ministry
- God-Honoring Stewardship
- Leadership Development
- Christ-Exalting Worship
- Disciple-Making Strategy
- Pastoral Leadership
- Loving Community
- Vision-Directed Systems
- Divine Enablement

Churches need to be flexible to adapt and stretch to embrace new challenges. The more flexible a muscle group, the less likelihood of injury. Likewise, the more flexible churches are, the more likely they will adapt to disciple-making opportunities. The characteristics that contribute to flexibility are loving community, vision-directed systems, and divine enablement. When the Spirit guides churches, when faith communities develop their systems and processes around vision, their agility and flexibility help avoid injury brought on by shortsightedness and stubbornness.

All twelve of these characteristics comprise the body composition of faith communities. In fitness terms, body composition is a "term for the percentage of fat, bone, and muscle in the body, of which fat is of greatest interest."[9] In general terms, the leaner the body mass, the more healthy/fit the individual. Balance is often the key. When the twelve characteristics are balanced in the life of churches, their body compositions become increasingly fit.

Joining the Run

This book explores the five types of churches in relation to each of the twelve characteristics of church fitness. It encourages church leaders to identify the type of church they serve, while providing practical guidelines for moving toward higher levels of fitness and, for a few, elite ministry.

Fitness requires measurements to track progress. The twelve characteristics of church fitness serve as a grid against which to compare the five types of churches. Descriptions and details of how the five types relate to each of the twelve characteristics are found in each chapter. As a church leader, you can quickly compare your church to the characteristic discussed.

In the areas where your church tracks well, you can rejoice. Where it does not track well, you learn the necessary adjustments to make to continue on the road to fitness.

The research foundation for this book comes from more than eighty years of combined experience in church leadership. Gary is a nationally and internationally respected writer, speaker, and professor and has focused on the biblical growth of churches for more than forty years. He is the author of twenty-five books and has published more than three hundred articles on a variety of topics related to church growth, pastoral ministry, and leadership. Phil has an extensive background in coaching denominational leaders, pastors, and church planters. He has consulted on church growth and multiplication issues with a variety of denominations and has conducted seminars all across North America on leadership, strategic change, church planting, church growth, evangelism, and missional church initiatives. He has spoken at conferences in North America, Australia, and Mexico and has written six books. Together, Gary and Phil bring a lifetime of research to bear in *Building the Body*.

Pursuing Fitness

Several years ago, Phil ran in a 5K event in his community. For this 5K run, like most others, organizers grouped runners into age categories. As Phil and his wife were watching the awards ceremony, they noticed a couple standing next to them. When the announcer read the name of the man next to them as the second-place winner in the sixty-plus age category, his wife said to him, "See, honey. I told you—if you live long enough, you win stuff." Church fitness is achievable, but it takes effort, energy, and equipping. In addition, the fitter the body, the greater its impact for Christ and his church.

Fitness is a lifelong pursuit for an individual or a church. When church leaders pursue fitness, they discover many benefits. What Phil discovered is he wanted to be fit, not a certain weight. Pursuing fitness, of course, has resulted in many additional benefits, including weight loss. How we attain fitness is one thing, and maintaining it is another. Either way, the pursuit continues.

Five core beliefs guide the move toward church fitness: (1) all fit churches are healthy, but not all healthy churches are fit; (2) fitness enhances overall health; (3) fit churches are missionally minded and externally focused; (4) fit churches are multiplying churches; (5) the primary motivator for moving from health to fitness is dissatisfaction.

Our goal in writing *Building the Body* is to help you understand and pursue fitness for your church. When you understand the benefits of being fit and are dissatisfied enough to begin running, a completely new world will open up for you and the

> *All fit churches are healthy, but not all healthy churches are fit.*

church you lead. Fit churches have more stamina. Fit churches have plans. Fit churches continually adjust to the world around them. Fit churches measure their progress. Thanks for choosing to go on this journey with us. You will not regret the run. Whether you are part of a beginner, a novice, an intermediate, an advanced, or an elite church, you can always achieve a level of fitness. Let's start running!

PART 1

CARDIOVASCULAR ENDURANCE

xygen is the lifeblood of the body. Oxygen is important to blood cells because it is necessary in making energy for our bodies. A body low on blood oxygenation functions at a much lower level. A healthy cardiovascular system delivers much-needed oxygen to the blood. Any activity that gets the heart beating faster contributes to an increased oxygen level. Running, skipping, walking, jumping rope, bouncing on a trampoline, or using an elliptical are examples of cardio-strengthening activities. Strengthening is not so much about *what* you do, as it is that you do *something*.

A strong church is built by developing strong cardiovascular systems. Fit churches need cardiovascular endurance to develop at a steady and sustained pace. It is cardiovascular endurance that provides the needed oxygen to produce energy in the church. Three functions that produce this energy for churches are outreach, effective evangelism, and community engagement. Each of these increases the cardiovascular levels of churches.

Outreach

You may have heard the phrase "If it were a snake, it would have bit me." People typically say this when they miss seeing something very close to them. It is common to look endlessly for an item only to discover it was right in front of you the entire time!

We are all guilty of this at one time or another. We go searching for an item, scour through drawers, shelves, closets, and then confidently declare, "I can't find it." Then to our chagrin, someone else looks and quickly discovers it. So why does this happen? Often the difference is simply focus. We think we are focused on finding the item, but our minds—our focus—are elsewhere.

An outward focus is the beginning point for outreach. Churches that are inwardly focused neither sense their communities' needs nor are motivated to evangelize or engage their communities. Outward-focused churches, however, are aware of the culture in which their ministries take place. They recognize a need for fitness to effectively evangelize and engage with their communities.

Church leaders often believe their churches are outward-focused when they actually are not. Many church people perceive themselves to be kingdom-minded, concerned for reaching the lost, and connected to people in their communities. Gary remembers consulting with a church in the Midwest. The results of a church-wide survey revealed several areas of strength and a few dominant weaknesses. One of the church's areas of strength was community outreach. Conversations in five focus groups revealed people believed their church was effective in reaching the community for Christ. Closer examination found otherwise. Five hundred dollars was budgeted for outreach but had not been spent in the past year. A full 99 percent of the church's identifiable programming was directed to the present congregation. The only identifiable program listed for outreach was VBS. The church was not outward-focused at all. How could a church be so wrong in its assessment of its strengths?

Sometimes the corporate ego generates such a false view. Churches can become like the person who says, "Well, enough about me, now tell me what you think about me." Other churches truly aspire to reach out, but the internal fellowship is so wonder-

---

You might be a fit and outward-focused church if . . .

- You designate 20 percent of your church budget for local outreach.
- You hold events in locations other than on your church property.
- You know the names of the business owners around your church location.
- You attend community functions.
- You discuss in all your board meetings how to reach your community.
- You talk about fulfilling the Great Commission more than about the property and facility issues.
- You see new people from the immediate community in your worship service.

ful the members forget those outside the church. This problem is so common among churches it is called "koinonitis." What are the symptoms? Koinonitis is present when those within the church become selfish. They wane in their desire to reach the unchurched. Their thinking, planning, and concern are all about them. At other times, perhaps most of the time, they just lack focus. Any outsider would find it painfully obvious that the church is not outward-focused, but no one inside the church can see it. Their vision is foggy and blurred.

Outward-Focus Infection

A short while ago, Phil's vision became a bit blurry. It wasn't enough to stop him from working, but it was distracting. An ophthalmologist examined Phil's eyes and determined an infection had attacked some of the nerve endings in one eye. The result? A foggy cornea. Eye drops and some oral medication restored his vision to normal.

The focus of churches can also become foggy, resulting in blurred vision. Churches may be able to function from day to day, but their blurred vision causes them to run off path. Churches desiring to build the body must be aware of potential infections that can disrupt their focus. Here are ten infections found regularly in churches. Check the box beside each one if you sense your church has its symptoms.

☐ *Missional Drift*

Churches can easily drift from the biblical purpose of fulfilling the Great Commission to the institutional purpose of surviving. They may begin to measure fruitfulness by the contentment of those in the pews. In reality, they ought to "constantly monitor [their] mission to bring the message of Jesus Christ to new generations and new cultures."[1]

☐ *Change Resistance*

Church researchers can agree with one pastor who writes, "A significant proportion of church leaders are content with the status quo."[2] Change must take place for a church to move from having an inward to an outward focus, but few leaders want to negotiate the process needed to initiate and implement that change.

☐ *Leadership Deprived*

A church needs a leader who is willing to show the way to the next level of effectiveness. "How can leaders expect their congregations to change if they themselves are unwilling to lead the way?"[3]

☐ *Overly Tolerant*

Churches may tolerate sin, infighting, complacency, and disruptive activity out of a misguided sense of acceptance. Clinical psychologist Henry Cloud states, "It's important for leaders to remember that they get what they tolerate."[4] The longer sin is tolerated, the deeper the rift. The deeper the rift, the stronger the hold on the church.

☐ *Functional Dysfunction*

When churches learn to function with their dysfunction, their dysfunction becomes the norm. It is their security. They know they're not what they can or ought to be, but they are comfortable. Many churches say they desire change but really do not. "Many churches never experience a comeback because they want the community to change while they remain the same."[5] The church becomes passive-aggressive. The church members may agree with a corporate nod, but they disagree with their actions.

☐ *Systems Suffocation*

Every church has systems in place. These systems guide the implementation of the church's mission and vision. Systems are necessary, but when the systems become the mission, the church suffocates. Systems are merely delivery methods for missions. Unfortunately, in many churches, the systems become the reason for the church existing. Churches can prevent systems suffocation by asking themselves a certain question. "Churches that operate by asking, 'What do you think we should do?' end up in a different place than churches that ask, 'What does God think we should do?'"[6] When churches ask God what ought to be done, systems are protected.

☐ *Cloudy Clarity*

Clarity in mission and vision is critical for the continued effectiveness of a church. Over time, clarity of direction may become cloudy, confusing, and downright chaotic. "Church leaders cannot expect folks to charge into the chaos of system change if they continue to sound such an ambiguous call."[7] Ambiguity (cloudiness) halts a church's effectiveness. Lack of clarity affects a congregation so that it either freezes and does nothing or it wanders off in the wrong direction.

☐ *Vision Indifference*

Communities of faith without a clear focus on their futures are on dangerous ground. "An exciting vision brings emotional fuel for change."[8] Indifference about the need to change is typically inward looking.

☐ *Inward Inertia*

Inward inertia occurs when "the focus of the church is on itself, not on what it takes to succeed."[9] Churches with this virus are often suffering from past hurt. Church splits, internal conflicts, or major disappointments may lead churches to turn inward to avoid further pain. An inward virus is difficult to combat. Only strong doses of spirit-filled antibiotics can bring such an infection under control and allow time for healing to occur.

□ *Success Cycle*

Churches that have had seasons of effective ministry tend to continue to do the same things they've always done. Past success, however, blinds people so they cannot see the current state of their churches. The culture of society has changed, yet past success makes churches refuse to adapt.

> The point is the world is profoundly different than it was at the middle of the last century, and everybody knows it; even the church culture. But knowing it and acting on it are two very different things. So far the North American church largely has responded with a heavy infusion of denial, believing the culture will come to its senses and come back around to the church.[10]

Inward-Focused Antibiotics

God made the human body to work in wonderful ways. Whenever our bodies come down with an infection, our immune systems jump into action. White blood cells stream throughout our bodies to find germs, latch onto them, and destroy them. In the most severe cases of infection, a doctor often prescribes antibiotics. Once inside our bodies, the antibodies find the germs causing the infection and wipe them out. Our immune systems strengthen, and if the same infection tries to enter our bodies in the future, our immune systems remember it and attack it with vigor. Experience is a good teacher, even when we are battling an infection.

The primary antibiotic used to defeat the infections that attack beginner churches is the *sent* nature of the church. Churches that do not grasp their *sentness* will wither in the call God has placed on their congregation. Churches will resist looking beyond themselves.

Before Jesus left his disciples, he clarified for them what he was sent to do and the call God had placed on his life (see John 16). Jesus would soon be arrested, tried, abandoned, crucified, buried, and eventually, resurrected. When he shared this with the twelve disciples, it was too much for them to grasp. They did not understand what he was wanting them to know (see vv. 16–28). Then they declared, "Now we understand" (John 16:30 NLT). Of course, he knew they really did not understand fully. How could they? They were about to enter one of the darkest times of their lives.

They would see him dead on a cross. The vividness of his death would extinguish their hope like a bucket of water poured on a lit match. Once hope is gone, discouragement, disengagement, and disinterest are not far behind. They could have easily compromised on their call. Their understanding was lost in the hollowness of Jesus's death. They needed prayer. A prayer to empower them once the realization of his resurrection shattered the reality of his death! They needed to be reminded they were missionaries (sent people), because he was a missionary (sent Savior). So Jesus prayed (see John 17).

Jesus's prayer clarifies missional (outward-focused) ministry. In this prayer, Jesus vividly portrayed the missional aspect of ministry: his own ministry, the twelve disciples' ministry, and our ministry.

The Missional Ministry of Jesus

God sent his Son into the world out of his love for the world (see John 3:16–17). God did this out of a heart of salvation, not condemnation. Jesus undergirded this in his prayer when he declared, "And this is eternal life, that they may know you, the only true God, and Jesus Christ whom you have sent" (John 17:3 NRSV). Jesus made clear that the strength of his followers was found in their understanding of his sentness. "Now they know that everything I have is a gift from you, for I have passed on to them the message you gave me. They accepted it and know that I came from you, and they believe you sent me" (John 17:7–8 NLT).

The Missional Ministry of the Twelve Disciples

Jesus's physical ministry on earth was limited to a three-year span. He was going to depart, leaving the disciples behind (see John 17:11). They would then need to take up the "sent" mantle. They were not going to be taken out of the world (see v. 15) but sent into it, as Jesus modeled for them. "As you sent me into the world," Jesus said, "I am sending them into the world" (v. 18 NLT). This is central to the ministry of those who follow Christ. It is an extension of the Father sending Jesus into the world.

The Missional Ministry of the Twenty-First Century

Jesus extends the same ministry to us today. The same prayer he prayed for his followers in the first century he prayed for us. "I am praying not only for these disciples but also for all who will ever believe in me through their message" (John 17:20 NLT). We are part of the *all* who will ever believe. It is our acceptance of the message! Our decision to believe should result in the same sentness of the first disciples. The time distance between us and the death and resurrection of Jesus does not negate the Great Commission.

The church has lost this missional (outward-focused) mentality. It has forgotten its mission is not about people coming to the church as much as the church going to people. When we go out, when we fully engage in being sent, we extend the ministry for which Jesus prayed. In a sense, our sentness makes us an answer to Jesus's prayers.

> I pray that they will all be one, just as you and I are one—as you are in me, Father, and I am in you. And they may be in us so that the world will believe you sent me. (v. 21 NLT)

> I am in them and you are in me. May they experience such perfect unity that the world will know that you sent me and that you love them as much as you love me. (v. 23 NLT)

> O righteous Father, the world doesn't know you, but I do; and these disciples know you sent me. (v. 25 NLT)

When we respond to our missional call, the world catches glimpses of Jesus. The church's willingness to go into culture is a singular clarion call to the reality of God! People best see and engage with God when his church goes out into the world.

Salvation is not an ending. It is a radical beginning.

It is the church acting in its sentness. Salvation is not an ending. It is a radical beginning. When we view salvation as our final destination, we negate our deep-felt gratitude. It is out of our gratitude that our call to serve springs. Service is more than an activity in which we engage. It is a responsibility in which we must immerse ourselves. Service is tangibly living out our sentness. And missional engagement is the earmark of a fit church.

Five Types of Churches

Beginner Churches

Beginner churches have little interest in the community or in the world around them. Leaders are focused on looking in the rearview mirror, not out the front windshield. Their concern is for survival, keeping the budget in the black, and maintaining peace in the congregation. While leadership gives a cursory nod to outreach, they do little to act. Outreach is an aspirational objective of these churches, but it is not an actionable objective.

PLAN OF ACTION IF YOU LEAD A BEGINNER CHURCH

- Read the Gospels, noting every time Jesus refers to being sent.
- Study Christ's prayer found in John 17.
- List five actions the church can take to move toward an outward focus.
- Pray specifically that God would open doors for outreach in the community.
- Allow the pastor to engage in community activities at least one hour per week.

Novice Churches

Novice churches have a selfish, inward focus but are beginning to take tangible steps toward an outward focus. Leaders recognize the nature of power. That is, the congregation will do what its leaders do. Thus, they are personally engaging in ministry outside the church's walls.

PLAN OF ACTION IF YOU LEAD A NOVICE CHURCH

- Identify actions your church can take to be more outward-focused.
- Select an action and carry it out.
- Allow the pastor to engage in community activities two to three hours per week.
- Encourage the pastor or key lay leader to teach a sermon series on John 17.

- Survey your church's people and find out who is actively engaged in community activities (e.g., team sports, school boards, service organizations, etc.).

Intermediate Churches

Intermediate churches see themselves as outward-focused. At least 10 percent of the members are involved in community activities. The pastors of these churches are active in at least one community group. Members understand the makeup of the community in which they reside.

PLAN OF ACTION IF YOU LEAD AN INTERMEDIATE CHURCH

- Encourage people to use spiritual gifts in the community, not just in the church.
- Equip people to be a spiritual presence in the community.
- Share stories of how church members are making a difference through serving in community activities.
- Make sure those on the church platform (e.g., preacher, worship team, worship/song leader, and any others who have a public presence) and in leadership roles (church boards and committees) reflect the community in which your church is present.
- Allow the pastor to engage in community activities four to six hours per week.

Advanced Churches

Advanced churches place a high value on their people being involved in community activities. They affirm ministry in the community as highly as ministry in the church. People on the church platform reflect the community in which the church resides. These churches expect and act as though new people are present in every meeting. Ministry training always addresses the community presence of believers.

Plan of Action If You Lead an Advanced Church

- Balance inside and outside ministry. Expect every member to have one ministry inside the church and one outside the church.
- Equip people to serve in the community.
- Measure effectiveness by how many people are involved in ministry outside the church.
- Allow the pastor to engage in community activities seven to ten hours per week.

Elite Churches

In elite churches, approximately 60 percent of congregants are involved in community-engagement activities. Every level of these churches' leadership is reflective of the community in which they are present. The pastors spend more than ten hours per week involved in community activities. They offer quarterly training to equip people to serve in the community. Elite churches constantly evaluate how to keep an outward focus. An outward focus is a core value, not merely an interest, and it is evident in the budget, ministries, and activity of the congregants.

Plan of Action If You Lead an Elite Church

- Build strategic partnerships with nonreligious community groups.
- Set a goal of having 60 percent of the church members engaged in strategic partnerships.
- Look for new means of keeping your outward focus.
- Allow the pastor to engage in community activities between eleven and fifteen hours per week.

Churches that are building the body work diligently to get, keep, and expand an outward focus. This outward focus becomes the epicenter of missional engagement. The result of an outward focus is improved cardiovascular endurance—the foundation on which effective evangelism and community engagement are built.

Main Points

- *Beginner church*: looks in the rearview mirror more than out the front windshield.
- *Novice church*: convicted of looking inward.
- *Intermediate church*: identifies as outward-focused.
- *Advanced church*: pushes people toward outward-focused ministries.
- *Elite church*: builds strategic partnerships with nonreligious community groups.

Effective Evangelism

Throughout North America and the world, we have found a hunger among church leaders to make an impact in their communities for the gospel. Church leaders want to be effective. They want to be kingdom outposts. They have a deep-seated desire to be the church God wants them to be. They want to be Holy Spirit–empowered, faith-filled, dynamic places of worship. They want to be the presence of Jesus in their part of God's kingdom. They want to be engaged in a positive way with those who are disconnected from Jesus.

Evangelism is one of the primary characteristics that help churches become fit. Evangelism provides oxygen to the body of Christ. New birth, growing believers, and an inflow of newly connected followers of Christ breathe life into faith communities.

Churches must be involved in evangelistic endeavors. Churches that do not make the effort to intentionally determine methods to share the gospel will erode in their fitness levels. Churches that do not involve themselves in an evangelical emphasis will

> **You might be a fit church if . . .**
>
> - You train and mobilize members to share their faith.
> - Your primary source of numerical growth is conversions.
> - You offer specialized opportunities for members to invite their friends.
> - You intentionally dedicate money and people to start new churches.
> - You regularly celebrate baptisms.
> - You identify and target unreached people in your community.
> - You give guests an opportunity to accept Christ in worship services.

find themselves aging with no kids or grandkids to carry on their legacy.

A Biblical Framework for Evangelism

Acts 1:8 contains the last recorded words of Jesus before his ascension. He said to his followers, "But you will receive power when the Holy Spirit comes upon you. And you will be my witnesses, telling people about me everywhere—in Jerusalem, throughout Judea, in Samaria, and to the ends of the earth" (Acts 1:8 NLT). In this verse, Jesus lays out four spheres of evangelistic ministry: Jerusalem, Judea, Samaria, and the ends of the earth (world).

These four spheres provide a strategic methodology for local church evangelism. Each sphere represents a specific aspect of evangelism.

Jerusalem implies a relational distinction. It is our personal sphere of influence. A sphere of influence is the circle of people an individual knows who are disconnected from Christ. Equipping people to share their faith stories is the best way to reach Jerusalem.

Judea is a geographical designation. Using the church's location as the center, draw a circle of one-fourth of a mile up to a five-mile radius. The radius is dictated by the population; the greater the population surrounding the church, the smaller the radius. Contextualized community engagement is the best way to reach Judea.

Samaria is both a geographical and a demographical designation. Samaria is the area that lies outside the geography of a church's particular Judea or a demographic either inside or outside your Judea that you are ill-equipped to reach. This ill-equipped status could be the result of language or cultural differences or a variety of challenges. Starting new faith communities is the best way to reach Samaria.

Ends of the earth speaks to the need to reach the entire world. Most often this points to the responsibility of churches to spread the gospel internationally. Doing so requires crossing borders. Sometimes the borders are actual geographical boundaries, but other times they are language, cultural, and worldview borders. The ends of the earth are best reached through the development of global partnerships.

Churches that are building the body have evangelistic processes and programs in each of these spheres. In this strategic model, evangelism begins in Jerusalem and flows outward to impact the world.

Effective Evangelism

Evangelism alone isn't all that matters—it must be *effective*. Churches cannot simply do evangelism; they must determine what form of evangelism is the most effective in each context. Effective evangelism is a means of presenting the gospel that connects with those you are attempting to reach. For example, a church on the north side of a community decided to do a complimentary hot dog and hamburger cookout in a local park. They did an excellent job promoting the event and hundreds of people showed up. As the people ate together, the church folks shared their personal faith stories. This evangelistic strategy proved to be very effective for this church.

When a sister church on the south side of town heard about the cookout, they liked the idea so much they decided to do the same thing. Organizers too set up in a park. They made sure they had plenty of hot dogs and hamburgers. They promoted well. The day came and very few people showed up. In fact, to their surprise, they received calls and posts on the church's Facebook page criticizing the event.

What happened? The south-side church neglected to get a feel for their community. You see, the community in which they were located was highly vegan. Therefore, the hot dog and hamburger cookout was not only unattractive but also downright offensive. Effective evangelism takes effort—and research.

Feather Flapping

Four guidelines can help to develop effective evangelism. These are guidelines, not programs. Regardless of your church's level of fitness, you can use these to craft effective evangelistic processes.

First, find your lift. For most of recorded history, people longed to be able to fly like birds. Over the years, as creative people considered how to get people off the ground and into flight, the natural bent was to imitate birds. People spent many hours observing birds in flight. Since birds use their wings to fly, a parade of people designed birdlike wings for people to wear, with unsuccessful results. Today we laugh at some of the early film of these attempts to fly. Trying to flap man-made wings just did not work.

This all changed when Swiss mathematician Daniel Bernoulli discovered "that as the velocity of a fluid increases, its pressure decreases."[1] Bernoulli's principle applies to any fluid, and since air is a fluid, it applies to air. In essence, his theory, when applied to flight, declared that "if the air speeds up the pressure is lowered. Thus the wing generates lift because the air goes faster over the top creating a region of low pressure, and thus lift."[2] His theory changed the conversation from feather flapping to lift—and lift is the force that holds an airplane in the air.

Each church must determine its evangelistic lift. Too often a church employs feather flapping. Two types of feather flapping are quite common. One occurs when a church adopts what another church is doing without adapting it to its own context. The second happens when a church looks for the plan-in-a-box. Both these approaches mimic the ministry of others. Unfortunately, most churches find that ministry by mimicry is mockery.

You need to do the difficult work of finding lift. You need to discover what will work in your community and be willing to understand the community in which God has placed your church. When you do this, when you find your lift, you will soar in evangelistic effectiveness.

Ministry by mimicry is mockery.

Second, resist the drill bit. Early in Phil's ministry, he discovered a useful principle called the "bit market." It was a principle birthed out of a parable. The story recounts a man who secures a job as a drill bit salesperson. The first day on the job the sales manager gives him some critical advice. The sales manager says, "When you go out to make your sales calls, remember this one thing—the market is for holes, not drill bits."

She goes on to explain that people and companies purchase drill bits to make holes. Their company sells holes. A market for holes will always exist but not necessarily a market for drill bits. If a better way comes along to make holes, then the company will sell that. The market is for holes.

Evangelism is a hole. Evangelistic drill bits are the methods used to drill the holes (evangelism). Door-to-door surveying, evangelistic crusades, the Four Spiritual Laws, confrontational evangelism, apologetic argumentation, lifestyle evangelism, bus ministry, and event-oriented outreach are examples of drill bits. You must resist the drill bit. Resist getting so locked into a certain type of method that you protect the drill bit at the expense of the hole. Effective evangelism focuses on the hole, not the drill bit.

Third, define the win. You will never know if you have won unless you know what it means to win. Golf is an excellent example. In most competitions, the team or individual with the highest point total wins. If you played a golf game with this perspective, you would seldom win. Why? A winner in golf has the lowest point total, not the highest. Not knowing this would place you at a huge disadvantage. Defining the win dictates the outcome.

When I (Phil) play golf, I have three criteria for a win: First, have a good time. Second, break one hundred in the number of strokes. Third, find more golf balls than I lose. Playing golf with this idea of a win determines my approach. My clearly defined outcomes allow me to enjoy the game much more than if I was to focus on making par.

As a church leader, you need to do the same to have effective evangelism. You need to define the win. The ultimate win is for people to come into a transformational relationship with Jesus Christ. Salvation, forgiveness of sin, and being restored in a relationship with God is what evangelism is about. Yet you have little control over this outcome. Jesus said in John 6:44, "For no one can come to me unless the Father who sent me draws them to me, and at the last day I will raise them up" (NLT). God draws people to him. Since it is "the Father" who draws people to himself, is counting decisions for Christ a win we have control over?

It is our contention that it is not. You need to define a win based on what you have control over. Here are two potential criteria for a win in effective evangelism: (1) Did you share the gospel in a clear, understandable manner? (2) Did you provide people an opportunity to respond to the gospel? If you are able to answer yes to these two questions, then you have effective evangelism. And the Father will draw them to him.

I (Phil) meet regularly with clusters of pastors for peer learning, encouragement, prayer, relationship building, and challenging one another to grow. Often I ask the pastors how many people came to Christ in the past month in their church. This question always encounters resistance as the pastors, rightly so, feel this is God's work, not theirs. When I hear this response, I retool my question and ask: How many times did you give people the opportunity to respond to the gospel?

A young pastor in one of the clusters was convicted by the Spirit. He realized he seldom gave people the opportunity to respond to the gospel. Without any public declaration to the group, he committed himself to giving people opportunities to respond. The next time we were together, he shared that as a result of presenting the opportunity for people to respond, four people had come to Christ.

The Father does indeed do the drawing, but usually you need to be the one to provide the opportunity for people to respond to the draw. Clarifying your win can make a huge difference in your approach and increase your evangelistic effectiveness.

Fourth, change. Sport psychology coach Rob Bell shares the following in his *Mental Toughness* blog.

Dick Vermeil became head coach of the St. Louis Rams in 1997 after a fifteen year absence from all of coaching.

He was infamous for 3 to 4 hour practices in full pads every day of the week.

He worked his players so hard that before one game in 1998 against the Bears, the entire team had a meeting about whether they should even play!

They had 9 wins in 2 years.

So, he changed . . .

He cut down practices to 1.5 hours no matter the situation and made sure his players were fresh heading into Sunday.

They won the Super Bowl in 1999. [3]

Those three words, *so, he changed,* are huge if you desire effective evangelism. What Coach Vermeil was doing was not working, so he changed. You need to regularly evaluate your evangelistic methods. How are you keeping the story fresh? How are you communicating the gospel? How do you determine if people understand the gospel? How are you equipping your church to be the gospel? If what you are doing is not working, then change!

Five Types of Churches

Beginner Churches

Beginner churches typically have no evangelistic processes in place. The people in these churches seldom invite others to church. These churches have an ingrown attitude. In many cases, even the pastor believes everyone who attends their church is already in a relationship with Christ. Gospel presentations are seldom, if ever, made. These churches are more concerned for those already in the body than those who remain outside the body.

These churches must begin with small initial steps toward effective evangelism. Too often an overzealous pastoral leader wants their church to be world-class in evangelism when the people have not shared the gospel in years. Such a church needs to get back to the basics.

Many people have stories about legendary National Football League coach Vince Lombardi. One story happened in the summer of 1961. At the beginning of training camp, Lombardi pulled together his Green Bay Packer squad. These were professional football players, many of whom had years of experience. But Lombardi did not want to take anything for granted. "He began with the most elemental statement of all. 'Gentlemen,' he said, holding a pigskin in his right hand, 'this is a football.'"[4] In beginner churches, you need to start with the basics.

PLAN OF ACTION IF YOU LEAD A BEGINNER CHURCH

- Encourage the pastor to teach a series on God's heart for those disconnected from him (e.g., Luke 15).
- Ask each person in the church to write down three to five names of people they associate with who may not know Jesus.
- Ask them to pray daily for those people throughout the year.
- Provide a small group or Sunday school book study on living life for Christ.
- Give people the opportunity to respond to the gospel during the service on two Sundays each month.
- Pray for those disconnected from Christ during prayer times.

Each element of this plan is low impact. The idea is to get those in beginner churches looking outward.

Phil was once working with a small church in Arizona that was averaging seventeen people in attendance. They had no one who had come to Christ in the past year. He asked the pastoral couple when was the last time they gave people the opportunity to respond to the gospel. They explained that it had been quite some time. They believed everyone in their church was already a Christian. "How do you know?" Phil asked.

He suggested the church follow a plan similar to the one suggested above. In the months following, they implemented the plan. Two people came to Christ as a result! It is better to help beginner churches take many small steps where they can succeed than attempt to get them to take a giant leap where they may fall.

Novice Church

Novice churches have begun to turn outward. Congregations are intentionally praying for friends and family disconnected from God. These churches are deeply aware that evangelism is the lifeblood for both their present and long-term health. They look for ways to express the gospel through relationships of integrity. They regularly present the gospel in worship services. People are given an opportunity to respond.

In novice churches, people are given tools to share their faith stories. Great Commission initiatives are consistently mentioned. But these churches are still a bit tentative. They have just begun their outward focus and, like a runner who is at the beginning stages of a fitness plan, novice churches can be a bit inconsistent in implementation.

PLAN OF ACTION IF YOU LEAD A NOVICE CHURCH

- Create systems of accountability for sharing faith stories.
- Set a goal for the number of weekends to present the gospel and give people the opportunity to respond.
- Develop a process to follow up with people who respond to the gospel.
- Recommend practical helps for people to practice being the presence of Jesus in culture.
- Offer Bible studies in public spaces (e.g., coffee shops, malls, parks).
- Have a framework for disciple-making.

A pastor friend was determined to get his congregation more outward-focused and to encourage them to share their stories outside the walls of the church. He designed a simple process that encouraged his folks to share their faith stories with others.

First, he taped a piece of butcher paper on one of the walls of the sanctuary (pretty fancy, right?). Second, he made felt pens available to use by the butcher paper. Third, he told his congregation that every time they performed an act of kindness in Jesus's name or prayed for someone's need (this prayer was not one of silence but done with the permission of the one being prayed for) or simply shared with someone their faith story, they were to place a mark on the butcher paper the following Sunday. Fourth, if they had thirty marks in any given month, they would have cake (who does not like cake?).

They did this for a year. They had cake every month. This exercise provided a foundation to build on for further effective evangelism.

Intermediate Churches

Intermediate churches have gained an evangelistic consistency not seen in novice churches. These churches have plans and strategies in place to equip the congregation in regular personal evangelism. Their worship experiences keep guests in mind at all times. Intermediate churches do everything possible to be welcoming to those foreign to the church experience. They offer many opportunities for people to get involved. Small groups connect people into the life of the faith community.

The downside of intermediate churches is that much of the connecting done in the community is designed to get people onto the physical church property. These are healthy churches that often become obsessed with their health. They tend to believe all fitness and health-oriented activity happens at the gym (church). Leaders equip people to engage others in the community, but every activity must end with the people coming to church. Often connecting people to the church becomes more important than connecting them to Christ. When connecting people to the church is viewed as the primary evangelistic purpose, church attendance can be seen as the end-all. The end-all is not involvement in a church—allowing Christ to be involved in each person's life is.

Plan of Action If You Lead an Intermediate Church

- Move toward a 60/40 approach to evangelism, with 60 percent happening off the campus and 40 percent on the campus.
- Equip people to share their faith through relationships, not simply through programs.
- Affirm ministry that takes place outside the walls of the church facility.
- Get involved in church planting in some manner.
- Invest finances in a struggling church.

Christmas Eve is typically a wonderful opportunity for people to come together and celebrate the birth of Christ. Congregations focus on remembering, often through communion, the source of their existence. Most of these gatherings conclude with the lighting of candles to remind the people they are the light of the world. In reality, this is an inward-focused, family-oriented event.

One church decided to add an unusual element to their Christmas Eve service. They added an offering—but not for them. Instead, they gave all the funds collected that night to a small, struggling church. Their offering was an extension of Christ to another. This simple act became a key aspect of helping this church continually look outside itself.

Advanced Churches

Advanced churches have made great strides toward effective evangelism. They have systems in place to reach and disciple others. Members are motivated to reach out with the gospel. Leaders are on the lookout for better and more effective ways to present the gospel.

Advanced churches are training churches. Leaders recognize the value of training members to connect with lost people. In light of the running metaphor, leaders seek a variety of terrain on which to train in order to expand the church's cardiovascular system.

Plan of Action If You Lead an Advanced Church

- Clarify your church's current level of evangelism fitness.
- Determine the next level of evangelism fitness to achieve.
- Decide what to do to move to the next level.
- Make sure your church has the information needed to move up.
- Do not fear your church being stretched out of its comfort zone.

Shoreline Community Church in Monterey, California, has worked diligently to equip people in living out the gospel in daily life. They teach the One-Degree Rule. "The One-Degree Rule acknowledges the reality that we need to increase our outreach temperature consistently."[5] By using a scale of 1–10 to determine evangelistic passion, the church has increased the desire of its members to share their faith stories with others. On the scale, one represents little interest in outreach, while a ten indicates a heart and passion for those disconnected from Christ. At all levels of the church, people are asked to rate themselves on the 1–10 scale. No one knows a person's outreach temperature but him or her. This makes it each person's responsibility to honestly assess themselves. Then they are to share how they will increase their temperature one degree. Using this basic tool allows the church to keep outreach on the front burner.

This is what advanced churches do—they find tools, methods, and resources and establish accountability markers to keep outreach on the front burner.

Elite Churches

Elite churches do many things well. Evangelism is focused on equipping the people to be Jesus in their contexts. They recognize that as involved as people may be in the ministry of the church, they spend most of their time away from the church. These churches consistently remind people they are God's investment where they are at any given time. They are missionaries in their neighborhoods, workplaces, schools, families, and communities. Elite churches celebrate salvations that happen outside the church building as much as, if not more than, those that happen inside the church.

Elite churches, like elite athletes, look to correct the small things. These churches consistently evaluate, review, and adjust what they are doing. They regularly engage others to look at how they can improve. Elite churches mobilize people to live like Jesus in their personal lives and as a corporate group together.

PLAN OF ACTION IF YOU LEAD AN ELITE CHURCH

- Resist complacency.
- Engage coaches and consultants on a regular basis.
- Find other churches in which to invest.
- Measure effectiveness by who your church sends, not who they seat.
- Compare your church to its potential, not what other churches are doing.

Katie Ledecky is an American swimmer. She is the current world-record holder in the 400-, 800-, and 1200-meter freestyle and has dominated the world in these events. She is an elite athlete.

When she swam in the semifinal heat of the 400-meter freestyle during the 2016 Rio Olympics, she was many lengths ahead of the field. She was so far out in front that it seemed as if she was the only one in the pool. She swam a great pace. How did she accomplish such a feat? She was not swimming against the others; she was swimming against herself.

This is what elite churches do. They worry less about what other churches are doing for the kingdom and more about what they should be doing. Church leaders push ahead to reach many with the gospel. Not to look better compared to other churches but to please the King.

Churches that are building the body are attempting to be effective in evangelism. Churches need to find how they can be effective in reaching others with the gospel. It is not the numerical size of the church but the passion of the church that matters.

Main Points

- *Beginner church*: low-impact evangelism.
- *Novice church*: baby steps into high-impact evangelism.
- *Intermediate church*: evangelism is getting people into the church.
- *Advanced church*: systems to raise evangelistic passion.
- *Elite church*: designs methods for effective evangelism.

COMMUNITY ENGAGEMENT

Community engagement is the third aspect of cardiovascular endurance. Cardiovascular endurance provides the oxygen necessary to supply energy to the muscles. Looking outward, equipping your people to share their faith stories, and reaching into your community supplies the oxygen to the body of Christ. Community engagement forces the church to interact with a world unlike itself.

The first-century church was in a very unwelcoming culture. Yet the church thrived. What the church today must not do is allow the culture to dumb down its message. And the church must still move into society.

The church must infiltrate culture as yeast does dough. This is the kingdom of God. "He also asked, 'What else is the Kingdom of God like? It is like the yeast a woman used in making bread. Even though she put only a little yeast in three measures of flour, it permeated every part of the dough'" (Luke 13:20–21 NLT). Through community engagement the church becomes

> **You might be a fit church if . . .**
>
> - You define your Jerusalem, Judea, Samaria, and the ends of the world (see Acts 1:8).
> - You meet with community leaders to discover how you might be able to help them.
> - You encourage church members to become involved in community activities, such as coaching youth sports, joining service clubs, becoming active in political forums, etc.
> - You study the community to determine what needs your church might be able to address.
> - You expect your pastor to spend part of the day in the community.
> - You engage in service evangelism activities in the community.
> - You are known for many positive contributions to your community.

like yeast. When the church embeds itself into the community in which it is located, transformation begins. When the church inserts itself in culture as Christ's representatives, things begin to change.

Three Approaches to Community Engagement

Churches must move into the culture in which they reside. The culture is exemplified by the community in which a church body finds itself. In the four spheres of evangelism mentioned earlier, this would be Judea. Judea is the geographical area stretching from a one-fourth to a five-mile radius around a church's meeting location. A fit church will engage the community in this geographic area.

Community engagement involves three basic approaches: attractional, missional, or connectional. These three approaches can be summed up in the following phrases: come and see (attractional); go and be (missional); go and bring (connectional).

54

Come and See

This approach focuses on bringing people through the church doors. Its emphasis is on attracting people. It is events-oriented and program-driven. The *come and see* approach is exemplified by:

- The church viewing itself as a purveyor of religious goods and services.
- The church bringing people out of the culture and into the church.
- The church prioritizing resources (time, energy, funds) on programs and property.
- The church focusing on increasing weekend participation and gaining members.

An example of a come and see approach to community engagement is found in a ministry popular some years ago called the "living Christmas tree." People from a church's choir sang traditional Christmas music while staged to look like a Christmas tree. Living Christmas trees were huge events used by many churches that attracted thousands of people each year. They consumed the energy of the entire church, and most enjoyed providing holiday entertainment for the community. The community enjoyed it too. Churches that used this program defined success as large crowds. It was a come and see approach to ministry.

Go and Be

The go and be approach to community engagement is to send people into the community. According to one pastor, "Our goal is not to get people 'in' our church, our goal is to equip people to go out from our church."[1] This approach is more missional than attractional. Churches that use this approach invest beyond themselves. They recognize that their work is about not only themselves but also the community in which God has placed them.

The go and be approach means churches actively serve in the community. This service dynamic is not designed to get those served into the church building. Instead, it is about getting the church out. "The simple approach of serving people in practical ways in the community is the most effective means of connecting your . . . church with the city where God has placed you."[2] This missional approach uses a different means of defining success. Success is tangibly living out the kingdom, not simply leading people into a church building.

The go and be approach is exemplified by:

- Sending people out of the church and into the community.
- Equipping people as missionaries for the culture in which they reside.
- Engaging people where they are, not where it is preferred they will be.

Lakeside is a suburb of San Diego. In this small community resides a church with a number for a name. This church is called *Seven*. This name was chosen to remind the people that the church is a seven-day-a-week venture. What happens on Sunday is not the only thing that makes the church the church. It is what happens through the people of Christ all throughout the week.

Missional thinkers and writers Hugh Halter and Matt Smay are convinced that "if you want to help people, we have to dive into people, wade into the sea of humanity."[3] This is the mindset of the go and be approach.

Go and Bring

As with most things in life, seldom do extremes fully satisfy. And community engagement is no different. The key to community engagement is often found in balance. It is finding that blend of coming in and going out.

In his article "The Goldilocks Rule: How to Stay Motivated in Life and Business," James Clear states, "Humans experience peak motivation when working on tasks that are right on the edge of their current abilities. Not too hard. Not too easy. Just right."[4] This is what a fit church is striving to do. Move to the edge of its current abilities and engage the community with a go and bring approach.

The go and bring approach is exemplified by:

- Mobilizing to be sent.
- Going into culture/community.
- Bringing people in.
- Building people up.
- Sending people out.

Chapter 1 of the Gospel of John contains a wonderful story that exemplifies the go and bring process of community engagement. Philip's life was drastically impacted by his encounter with Jesus. As a result of this encounter, "Philip went to look for Nathanael and told him, 'We have found the very person Moses and the prophets wrote about! His name is Jesus, the son of Joseph from Nazareth.' 'Nazareth!' exclaimed Nathanael. 'Can anything good come from Nazareth?' 'Come and see for yourself,' Philip replied" (John 1:45–46 NLT).

Philip went to look for Nathanael. He did not extend an invite to meet him someplace. Philip went to Nathanael. This is *going*. He engaged Nathanael where he was. He shared his story using a common connection. It was only after this that Philip invited Nathanael to join him. This is *bringing*.

The go and bring approach views the location of the faith community as a hub of strengthening Christ followers to be sent out. The church is both gathered and scattered. "Let's start living out the AND and be the gathered community of God's people, sent out into the world."[5] Let the church engage the community!

Cultivate Your Judea

An error many pastors make is to assume that having a building in a community makes them present in the community. Your property is not your presence in the community. Your engagement in the community is your presence. You can be present in a community without having a presence in the community.

Phil and his wife had the privilege of being a part of a team that launched a new church in McCordsville, Indiana. McCordsville is a bedroom community east of downtown Indianapolis. The baby church had no building or property. Thus, like many new churches, it met in a local school on Sunday mornings.

Your property is not your presence in the community. Your engagement in the community is your presence.

Phil had the ministry of signs and wonders, which meant he assembled a team that put out signage (signs) to help direct newcomers to the worship service. Due to city regulations, the church could not put out signs until Friday afternoon. And the signs needed to be down by Sunday evening. Therefore, the church's signs appeared and disappeared (wonders) each weekend. If the church had depended on its weekend physical presence for its sole community presence, it would have been ineffective. The church members had to go out into the community.

The following eight guidelines will be helpful in developing a community engagement strategy. Based on the four spheres of evangelism, we will use Judea as the designator for your community.

First, identify your Judea. As stated earlier, Judea is a geographical designation. Using the church's location as the center, draw a circle of one-fourth of a mile to a five-mile radius. The radius is dictated by the population; the greater the population, the smaller the circumference. Contextualized community engagement is the best way to reach Judea.

Second, understand your Judea. This is a demographic identification. You can exegete your Judea both formally (demographic studies) or informally (drive or walk around in your Judea, ask questions, observe, connect with the local chamber of commerce).

Third, understand your church. This is an internal audit. Ask questions. How many people currently attending the church live in your Judea? How reflective is your congregation of your Judea? What has your church done previously to engage Judea? Gary often notes that if the average age of the congregation is ten years or older than the people living in the community, there will be a disconnect. Keep this in mind as you attempt to better understand your church.

Fourth, inventory your resources. Your resources are the people, finances, ideas, professions, skill sets, and abilities of those in the congregation.

Fifth, determine the needs in your Judea.

Sixth, decide on your course of action. The key question: What can you do in, and for, your community that if you were no longer present, your presence would be missed?

Seventh, mobilize the church.

Eighth, evaluate your effectiveness. What results can you observe? What needs to be changed, adapted, or discontinued?

Community engagement is best birthed through relationships. In his book, *The Celtic Way of Evangelism*, George Hunter suggests the single most significant insight that can be garnered from how Saint Patrick reached Ireland is that of relational understanding. "The fact that Patrick understood the people, their language, their issues, and their ways, serves as the most strategically significant single insight that was to drive the wider expansion of Celtic Christianity."[6] You will never fully engage your community until you step fully into the culture.

Contextualize; Do Not Compromise

One of the biggest hurdles to community engagement is the fear of compromise. This fear is especially heightened when the culture in which the church finds itself is perceived as adversarial. This perception can result in the church withdrawing into a fortress mentality. Then the church becomes about *protecting* itself instead of *projecting* into the community it is to reach. Concern over compromise may cause a church to withdraw and focus on things other than the gospel.

How a church responds to the community flows out of the purpose it sees itself fulfilling. An example can be borrowed from the contrast between Eastern monasteries and Celtic monastic communities. Eastern monasteries were designed to protect against and escape from the sinfulness of Roman culture. These monasteries were for withdrawal and located off the well-worn tracks of everyday life. They were populated by monks searching inward at the expense of outward seeking. Soul protection took precedent over soul provision.

Contrast this to Celtic monastic communities. "The Celtic monasteries organized to penetrate the pagan world and to extend the church."[7] They were developed to save souls; therefore, they were constructed in easy-to-find locations. The Celtic monasteries were for pushing out, not pulling in.

A church that is serious about moving toward an elite status must push into uncomfortable realms. This will dictate that the means and the message be contextualized. "The first phase of any mission must involve *cultural engagement*. Engagement of culture may *sound* like evangelism, but it is really about 'context.'"[8] The core of contextualization over compromise is the centrality of the gospel.

In Acts 15, we see the early church in a state of tension. The gospel was flowing from a Jewish context into a Gentile world. The acceptance of the gospel by Gentiles forced the primarily Jewish church to adjust and align. When you move toward community engagement, you will need to adjust and align (contextualize) without losing sight of the gospel (compromise). How did the early church balance this?

- Contextualization never dilutes the joy of salvation. Conversions are celebrated (v. 3). Gentiles were coming to Christ and this caused joy.
- Contextualization demands conflicts be addressed thoughtfully and honestly (vv. 5–6). The conflict point in the early church was the demand of some that Gentiles be both converted and circumcised (v. 5). Instead of making a snap judgment, the leaders met to resolve the matter together (v. 6). Contextualization is doing the difficult work of conflict resolution.
- Contextualization is filtered through the gospel, not personal preference (vv. 8–11). The bottom line is that the Gentiles were given the Holy Spirit (v. 8), they were cleansed by faith (v. 9), and salvation was given by grace (v. 11). When criteria other than the gospel are used, compromise will follow.
- Contextualization is based in Scripture (vv. 15–18). The higher view you have of Scripture, the greater your defense against compromise.
- Contextualization finds common ground in the life-transforming message of Jesus (vv. 28–29). Common ground is that which edifies the church, builds up the believer, and honors Christ.

When a church makes the determination to engage the culture, it risks its reputation. There is never any guarantee the community and/or culture will not influence the church more than the church influences the culture. But it is worth the risk.

Five Types of Churches

Beginner Churches

Beginner churches must start with what they can do. Your church may not know anything about the community. You may have limited resources. The best place to begin is where you are.

When Phil got serious about his personal fitness, he had no *chic* running equipment. All he had was tennis (not running) shoes, old gym shorts, and a T-shirt. He had not been on a run or an extended walk in years (literally years). Instead of waiting to get what he wanted, Phil decided to start with what he had.

You have to crawl before you walk; you have to walk before you run; and you have to run at a pace you can manage, or you will quit running. Phil began his fitness journey by walking ten minutes at a time. The pace he walked was irrelevant. The time he walked was what mattered. Gradually he began to add one minute each time he walked until he built up to walking for thirty minutes. Beginner churches must start engaging their communities in a similar manner, no matter how small the first steps. Then, over time, they can increase their level of engagement.

PLAN OF ACTION IF YOU LEAD A BEGINNER CHURCH

- Define your church's Judea.
- Communicate Judea to your church.
- Pray for your church's Judea.
- Design and implement a prayer walk/drive for your church's Judea.
- Sit weekly in key public spaces in your Judea. Observe and take notes.
- Make a list of five needs in the community.
- Select one need your church can meet.
- Determine a way to meet the need.

Novice Churches

Novice churches are just beginning to become active in their communities. They are getting out and walking—and mixing in some running as well. The distance they can go is short but manageable. That's fine, because novice churches need to work at a pace they can handle.

Once Phil had built up to a thirty-minute continuous walk, he began to run a bit in addition to walking. His time frame was the same (thirty minutes), but he would walk for five minutes, run for two minutes, and repeat. Phil needed to ease into more vigorous activity. His goal was to be able to run for a continuous thirty minutes. Once he could do that, he would then track the number of miles.

PLAN OF ACTION IF YOU LEAD A NOVICE CHURCH

- Meet with key community leaders (e.g., school principal, police chief, fire chief, mayor, chamber of commerce president) and ask them for a list of the needs in the community.
- Determine a need your church will meet.
- Survey your church's resources.
- Build a team to meet the community need.
- Have your church focus on the need and do all it can to meet the need.
- Evaluate how effective your church is at meeting the need.

Intermediate Churches

Intermediate churches are consistently engaging their communities in several ways. They are building up endurance and beginning to develop a faster pace. Community engagement begins to expand to a wider variety of ministries.

Phil got to the point where he was running for thirty consecutive minutes. Then he began to add speed to increase his endurance. As his pace increased, so did his overall endurance.

PLAN OF ACTION IF YOU LEAD AN INTERMEDIATE CHURCH

- Look for additional needs in the community that your church can meet.

- Make community engagement an expectation for your church's members.
- Increase your church's budget for community engagement activities.
- Identify a leader who can mobilize more people for community engagement.

Advanced Churches

Advanced churches have a high level of community influence. They maintain a variety of community engagement ministries. Community engagement is part of their DNA.

Phil had increased his running stamina to the point that he was running from thirty to forty minutes at an eight-minute-per-mile clip. While this pace would not break any world records, it was excellent for him. He began to look for longer races in which to compete, and he eventually ran a half marathon.

Plan of Action If You Lead an Advanced Church

- Multiply leaders who can manage groups in community engagement.
- Encourage and expect the people to generate community engagement ideas.
- Expect every ministry group in your church (e.g., youth, women, men, small groups) to make community engagement an aspect of what they do.
- Encourage the people to serve on community boards, coach athletic teams, participate in school leadership, and volunteer in any other arenas where they can be salt and light.

Elite Churches

Elite churches put in the work; they are totally absorbed in community engagement. They measure effectiveness by a much higher standard than others and push themselves relentlessly to do better.

Phil is not an elite runner. Few people are. Elite runners train tirelessly, and in their efforts to be the best runners possible, they run dozens of miles each week. Running is the core of who they are. They build their lives around getting fitter, better, faster.

Plan of Action If You Lead an Elite Church

- Increase the percentage of people involved in community engagement.
- Consistently ask what else your church can be doing to engage the community.
- Train other leaders how to engage their communities.
- Start churches in areas your church is not effectively reaching through community engagement.

One of the best questions leaders can ask about their churches is this: When all is said and done, what will be said about what was done? This question forces you to evaluate what you are doing. It's an excellent question for church leaders to ask *and* answer while building the body. The answer you provide will determine the actions you take.

Main Points

- *Beginner church*: seeks the heart of God for the community (Judea).
- *Novice church*: finds one need to meet.
- *Intermediate church*: makes community engagement a membership expectation.
- *Advanced church*: imbeds community engagement into the DNA of the church.
- *Elite church*: plants churches with community engagement in their DNA.

PART 2

MUSCULAR
STRENGTH

Muscular strength is the highest amount of effort exerted by the muscles of the body to overcome the most resistance in a single effort. Muscular strength influences everything the body does—from getting out of bed in the morning to getting back in bed at night and everything in between. All activity requires muscular strength. Churches need muscular strength to overcome the resistance society exerts against them. They need muscular strength to serve their communities, to preach the gospel, and to build up their members. Personal ministry, God-honoring stewardship, and leadership development provide muscular strength. Each of these characteristics strengthens the spiritual muscles needed for a church body to be fit.

Personal Ministry

The eloquent witness of Scripture points out the reality of what we might call "people power." Even a cursory glance through the Bible illustrates this truth. God used Adam, Enoch, Noah, Abraham, Isaac, Jacob, Joseph, David, Hannah, Deborah, Solomon, and Elijah in the Old Testament. He used Peter, Paul, Luke, Lydia, Priscilla, Apollos, Timothy, Titus, Aquila, and John in the New Testament. And, of course, we easily think of many servants who came later, such as William Carey, Martin Luther, John Calvin, Dwight L. Moody, Billy Graham, and Ed Schneider.

Ed Schneider! Who is Ed Schneider? He was Gary's youth leader, of course. You most likely do not know him, but he is representative of uncountable numbers of people God has used to further his cause over some two thousand–plus years. At the time, Ed was serving as a soldier in the US Army. Later, after he left military service, he worked as a loan agent for a local loan company. Ed was not a seminary graduate. He was not formally ordained. He was not employed full time in a paid ministry position. Ed reminds us, however, that God acts through all his

---

You might be a fit church if . . .

- You teach and preach on spiritual gifts.
- You help people discover their unique purpose in ministry.
- You equip people to use their gifts, talents, and skills in ministry.
- You place people in ministry according to their passions.

- You provide encouragement through coaching of those in ministry.
- You offer ongoing training for people to improve their ministry skills.
- You express appreciation in various ways to those involved in ministry.

---

people, working in concert with the Head—Jesus Christ. People power was evident in the life of Ed Schneider due to his willingness to use his gifts in sacrificial service to the Lord he loved.

Foundations for Personal Ministry

A vital belief of any fit church is that God uses his people to grow his church.

The Great Commission states Christ's followers are expected to propagate the faith. We are all to be "witnesses" (Acts 1:8), all to use our gifts (see 1 Pet. 4:10), all to do the work of ministry (see Eph. 4:12). God does not call to ministry only a few highly gifted people. Instead, he calls all his people to serve him in his mission in the world.

The Church—a Kingdom of Priests

The true followers of Jesus Christ are called priests. The apostle John wrote to the early churches, "He has made us to be a kingdom, *priests* to His God and Father—to Him be the glory and the dominion forever and ever. Amen" (Rev. 1:6, emphasis added). Peter likewise understood the high standing of God's people. "And coming to Him as to a living stone which has been rejected by men, but is choice and precious in the sight of God, you also, as living stones, are being built up as a spiritual house for a *holy priesthood*, to offer up spiritual sacrifices acceptable to God through Jesus Christ" (I Pet. 2:4–5, emphasis added). The church—a kingdom of priests!

This priesthood of all believers is a commonly agreed on doctrine (at least among Protestant churches), but it continues as a work in progress. Christians still struggle with the meaning of their divinely ordained title. Many Christians have never seriously sought to find a personal place in the priesthood of all believers. Nevertheless, the proper starting point for engaging believers in personal ministry is a biblical understanding of those who are members of a church.

The Priests—a People

The church is one class of people. The historical division of God's people into two classes—clergy and laity—is unfortunate. The term "laity" (*laos*) derives from the Greek word for people, crowd, or nation. It designates those who belong to the people of God. For example, Paul told Titus he was looking for the blessed hope and appearing of Christ Jesus, "who gave Himself for us to redeem us from every lawless deed, and to purify for Himself a *people* for His own possession, zealous for good deeds" (Titus 2:14, emphasis added). The true laity are all those who have been chosen by God, called out of the mass of humankind, and are following him. The idea of a separate clergy (*kleros*) class of people is not in the Bible. Evidently, the idea of a separate class of trained people called "clergy" came from Greco-Roman politics and slowly made its way into church language and practice. Yet the Bible contains no glimmer of the idea of a separate class of clergy versus laity. There is only one class of people—the people of God. The biblical words for God's people are *disciples, Christians,* and *saints* (see Acts 11:26; Eph. 2:19). We are all one people.

The People—Ministers

God's people are called and gifted to serve him. The apostle Peter declares that each believer "has received a *special* gift" and that we should "employ it in serving one another as good stewards of the manifold grace of God" (1 Pet. 4:10). According to Paul, "We have gifts that differ according to the grace given to us," and we should exercise them accordingly (Rom. 12:6). Speaking about spiritual gifts to the Corinthian believers, Paul writes, "Each one is given the manifestation of the Spirit for the common good" (1 Cor. 12:7). Even though good works do not save us (see Eph. 2:8–9), God has created us for good works and expects us to do them (see v. 10).

The Pastors—Teachers and Trainers

Some of the people of God rise up to become leaders. Paul points out at least four (possibly five) leadership roles among God's people: apostles, prophets, evangelists, pastors, and teachers (see Eph. 4:11). The role of these leaders is not to do all the work of ministry but to train the people to do God's work. Those called apostles, prophets, evangelists, pastors, and teachers are to equip the saints "for the work of service" (v. 12). "To equip" is used in the Greek language in the sense of setting a broken bone or mending a torn net. Essentially, it connotes the idea of making a person or object fit to do the task for which they were created. Thus, a net is mended so it can be used to catch fish. A broken leg bone is set so the leg can function properly. Therefore, church leaders are to train the people of God to make them fit to do the work for which Christ called them. This means (among many other things) apostolic church leaders are to train people to plant churches, prophetic leaders are to teach people to declare God's Word, evangelistic leaders are to train God's people to reach nonbelievers, pastoral leaders are to train people to protect and care for others, and teachers are to train people to understand and obey God's Word.

The Gifts—Building Up the Body

We define personal ministry as accomplishing the purpose of the church through the members of the church. The overarching reason for training people to use their God-given gifts is "to the building up of the body of Christ" (Eph. 4:12). This "building up" spans the entire scope of growth: personal maturity, spiritual growth, and numerical expansion of the church. "We are to grow up in all aspects into Him who is the head, even Christ, from whom the whole body, being fitted and held together by what every joint supplies, according to the proper working of each individual part, causes the growth of the body for the building up of itself in love" (Eph. 4:15–16).

Build Momentum for Personal Ministry

Becoming a fit church is directly proportional to the degree the people of God are active in ministry. This principle has significant implications for a local church. Among other things, it means the heartbeat for a local church is the training of its people. Fit churches do the following things.

First, fit churches train people to know their spiritual gifts. People's identities as gifted servants of God are important impetuses for involvement in ministry. Classes and small group leaders systematically teach that God calls his people to serve. As each person grows to understand their identity in Christ and his body, they catch the vision of personal ministry. Each one identifies their remarkable spiritual gifts, unique talents, and special skills. They discover their passion for ministry while committing to serving with the rest of the church body.

Second, fit churches equip people to use their gifts, abilities, and skills in ministry. As the consciousness for personal ministry develops within the church body, the church offers training to help people develop needed skills. The church begins by determining the needed skills in the community and the church. One church determined it needed to train people to share Christ with the nonchurched community. Another decided to train people to minister care to those in need. Still another organized a training event for tutors of elementary school–age children. Training does not necessarily mean a church must have a full-blown curriculum or training classes. The easiest way to begin is simply to ask those currently involved in church ministry to find an apprentice. As each person recruits and begins meeting with an apprentice, training begins naturally. The total number involved in personal ministry doubles. A church may certainly decide to provide a more formal training environment, but it is not necessary to do so to get started. The training does not need to be elaborate; it needs only to be functional.

Third, fit churches place people into ministry—quickly. Gary remembers how God started using him during his high school years. After becoming a Christian at age fourteen, Gary attended his church's youth group for the first time. The next week, the leader of the youth group asked Gary to lead the music. The very next week! Gary had been involved in music since third grade, but he literally knew none of the songs the youth group sang. The youth director took a chance on Gary, and by getting him involved soon, the director communicated the importance of service—and Gary has been involved in ministry ever since!

In contrast to Gary's experience, consider how differently many churches approach recruiting people to serve. Most make the new person observe the church's ministry for a period of time. Later, when church leaders try to get the newer person involved, they find resistance. Why? The church has actually trained the new person to sit and be served rather than to work and serve others.

A church must be wise (we do not want new people teaching our children doctrine), but engaging new people to serve in ministry early on pays rich dividends later. Fit churches typically have many entry-level options that allow newcomers to serve right away.

Fourth, fit churches provide coaching for people in ministry. Formal coaching is a somewhat recent development in churches, but people placed in ministry positions must always have someone of whom they can ask questions. One major advantage of an apprentice model is that it has a built-in coaching connection. In other situations, a coach can be assigned to a person in ministry. Whatever a church decides to do, it is important that no new servant be left alone.

A key part of Gary's story is that he was coached. When Gary occasionally said something distracting while leading music, the youth leader would suggest a better way to make transitions between songs. He never corrected Gary in front of the other youth; he always waited to do it privately. However, when Gary did a fine job of leading, the youth director praised him in front of the other youth, thereby raising Gary up as a leader in their eyes.

Fifth, fit churches evaluate people in ministry. A coach should contact a person newly placed into ministry every week for one to two months. After the new person has two months of fruitful experience, a coach may reduce contact to around once a month. Coaching time should focus on questions such as "How are things going?" "What problems are you encountering?" "What further training would be beneficial?" "Are you experiencing a positive level of success?" The coach should address whatever issues they discover. If the person is not happy or not experiencing some level of success, the coach should attempt to place them in another ministry.

Sixth, fit churches build new ministry around their people's gifts and passions. New people bring new gifts, skills, and interests to a church. In growing churches, the increase in the number of people reveals the need for fresh ministries and approaches. For example, a church may have one family with a child with special needs, but the church is too small to meet those needs. A larger church may discover fifteen families in the church have children with special needs. With such a critical mass, such a church may find it also has new people skilled to design and run a ministry for those children. The same is true for numbers of other needs and interests. The larger a church grows, the more it must be starting new ministries that serve the new people.

Seventh, fit churches express thanks to those in ministry. Churches that successfully enroll people in ministry over a long period of time have several ways of saying thanks to them. One church hosts a catered "Dinner of Appreciation" every year in May to which they invite people who have served in a ministry during the previous twelve months. A pastor in a smaller church handwrites one thank-you note a week to someone serving in ministry. He systematically works his way through every person in service and then begins over again. One church holds an awards dinner each year and distributes fun awards, such as the Golden Banana Award (for the most creative new ministry), the High Dive Award (for the most daring action taken by someone in ministry), and the Crazy Clown Award (for the person in ministry who makes everyone laugh). A church in Southern California allows its pastor to spend 1 percent of the church's budget as he desires to motivate people. He often gives people checks along with thank-you notes with directions such as "Take your husband out for dinner for me." Still other churches give out gift cards to local coffee shops as tokens of appreciation.

Be Sensitive to People's Expectations

Competition for people's time and energy has never been as intense as it is today. Work schedules, youth commitments, and leisure activities compete head-to-head for people's involvement. So how can churches attract people to become involved in ministry? One way is to be sensitive to the expectations of people who serve.

First, people expect personal invitations to participate in ministry. Once upon a time, a pastor could simply announce a church's need for help from the pulpit and people would respond. In today's competitive environment, however, people expect the church to invite them personally to serve.

Second, people expect the church to prepare and equip them for ministry assignments. Invitations to serve must come with the opportunity to receive training for the job. People resist taking a position they are simply thrown into.

Third, people expect follow-up, encouragement, and recognition. Once a person accepts a new assignment and begins working, they look for regular evaluation and encouragement. People do not like Lone Ranger roles with no contact from leaders.

Fourth, people expect service opportunities that fit their schedules. People respond to ministry opportunities that provide a choice of times. While people want to serve, they must fit the ministry into their already busy schedules. The more you can offer choices for times and days they can serve, the greater the chance they will become involved.

Fifth, people expect to use their unique skills and personalities in a meaningful manner. People understand God has uniquely gifted them, and they desire to use those gifts. Thus, the more your church can tie invitations to serve to people's spiritual gifts, the greater the chance they will agree to serve.

Sixth, people expect to make a difference in their churches, communities, and the world. Serving in a significant way is important to people. They make decisions about how to use their time, in part, based on their perceived value of the opportunity. The church has the greatest mission in the world, but leaders must communicate how each ministry opportunity fits into the Great Commission. The more people can see the important value of their roles, the more likely they are to serve.

Seventh, people expect to build relationships. After over thirty years of research, it's clear that the number-one reason people participate in ministry is the friendships they develop through serving. Building teams around the numerous areas of service in your church is a good way to bond people together for fruitful ministry.

Eighth, people expect to grow spiritually and personally. Ministry burnout must be avoided at all costs. People who agree to serve in your church's ministry want to experience growth spiritually and personally through their service.

Ninth, people expect their personal needs to be met. Leaders who oversee ministry workers must be sensitive to the needs of those who serve with them. Leaders must be shepherds, not only managers. Caring for workers involves listening to their hurts, problems, and needs. The more you care for your workers, the more they will care for the work.

Five Types of Churches

Beginner Churches

Beginner churches find it difficult to recruit people to serve. Their recruitment strategy is often to pray that trained workers from other churches join their church in the future. They do not allow new people to serve unless they have a long history of service in another church. The pastor or key ministry leaders are usually responsible for recruitment, leaving the church suffering from the proverbial problem of only 10 percent of the people doing 90 percent of the work.

PLAN OF ACTION IF YOU LEAD A BEGINNER CHURCH

- Lead the church board in a study of the people of God in the Bible, particularly highlighting their important place in God's work.

- Develop a class or small group study on spiritual gifts and begin teaching it to 10 percent of the church's adults each year for the next five years.
- Ask the pastor to teach or preach on the stewardship of time, treasures, and talents.
- Visit and talk with other churches that have an effective ministry placement program.
- Complete an audit of the church's current ministry involvement to have a record of what is actually happening. Look for answers to the following questions: How many ministry jobs are currently available? How many are filled? How many are focused on ministry inside the church to present members? How many are focused outside the church to potential members? How many, and what percentage, of your people are actually involved in a ministry? How many, and what percentage, are not involved?

Novice Churches

Novice churches have never given serious consideration to using new people, and of course, only a few if any entry-level areas of service are available for new people. Sermons or classes in the past have focused on the topic of spiritual gifts but have produced no lasting benefit to the number of people serving in the church. However, the pastor does exhort people from the pulpit to use their spiritual gifts, but few understand how to use them. Those who desire to serve cannot find a clear pathway to do so. Members are often heard complaining that only 20 percent of the people are doing 80 percent of the work.

PLAN OF ACTION IF YOU LEAD A NOVICE CHURCH

- Encourage the pastor to preach or teach a series on spiritual gifts.

- Do an inventory to discover what ministry positions are available, highlighting vacant positions.
- Make a list of all the people in your church, clearly marking those who are serving and those who are not.
- Offer a class on discovering your gifts and passions for ministry and invite people who are not currently involved in any ministry.
- Try to match the people in the class to one of the unfilled positions on your church's list.

Intermediate Churches

Intermediate churches have started to take seriously the teaching, training, and recruiting of people based on their spiritual gifts. They've made a number of attempts to train and equip people for service, but the church is still seeking a workable system. The attempts have produced some results, and about 30 percent of attendees are involved in an aspect of personal ministry. Newcomers are allowed to serve in low-level ministry positions. However, only relatively few entry-level jobs are available.

PLAN OF ACTION IF YOU LEAD AN INTERMEDIATE CHURCH

- Make a list of all the ministries your church offers and indicate the entry-level ones in which newcomers might be allowed to serve.
- Invite people who have been in your church for less than two years to participate in a class or small group training to discover their gifts and passions for ministry.
- Encourage those in the class or small group to volunteer for the entry-level positions.
- Develop a leadership ladder that shows all the available positions in the church from the lowest entry-level positions

at the bottom (such as parking attendants) to the positions at the top (such as elders).

- Design a clear pathway from the bottom of the ladder to the top. That is, outline the steps a new person might take to work their way from the bottom to the top.

Advanced Churches

Advanced churches have developed and are using effective systems for recruiting, training, and deploying people in ministry. They have articulated clear pathways to service, which they publish widely in brochures and on the church's website. The church has assigned to a pastor the responsibility of helping people discover and use their spiritual gifts. At last count, the church has around 40 percent of its people serving in some form, both inside and outside the church.

PLAN OF ACTION IF YOU LEAD AN ADVANCED CHURCH

- Organize a Ministry Placement Team (MPT) and give them responsibility to develop a complete ministry pathway for your church.
- Appoint a ministry leader to be responsible for the MPT.
- Develop a ministry pathway for the church that clearly describes and visually shows how to get involved in ministry service.
- Publicize the pathway to ministry service in brochures and on the church's website.
- Develop a plan to recruit and train every member of the church for service. Systematically work through the entire list of attendees until the church has successfully trained two-thirds of its people. After one year, evaluate the pathway to ministry service and make adjustments to improve it.

Elite Churches

Elite churches have clear pathways to service, as well as very workable systems to place people in ministry. Newcomers understand how to get involved in service and find it easy. Numerous classes and/or small groups offer training for people to understand their gifts and passions for ministry. Churches provide wide ranges of service opportunities and large numbers of entry-level ministries for newcomers. They also help people understand their gifts and find them places to serve. Over 50 percent of people serve in some ministry role.

PLAN OF ACTION IF YOU LEAD AN ELITE CHURCH

- Hire a full-time pastor of ministry placement to oversee the entire recruitment, training, and placement process for the church's ministries.
- Identify unique areas of people's needs and giftedness and begin new ministries to fit them.
- Dedicate 5 percent of the total church budget to ministry placement.

Main Points

- *Beginning church*: does not use spiritual gifts in any significant manner.
- *Novice church*: teaches spiritual gifts but does not employ them in ministry.
- *Intermediate church*: uses gift-based ministry, but there is limited opportunity for new people.

- *Advanced church*: a Ministry Placement Team is functioning to recruit, train, and deploy people into gift-based ministry.
- *Elite church*: gift-based ministry is fully functional at every level of the church body.

GOD-HONORING STEWARDSHIP

How people and churches handle money declares the kingdom to which they belong. Jesus laid out two options. We can either store up treasures for ourselves on earth or store up treasures for ourselves in heaven (see Matt. 6:19–20). He also said, "No one can serve two masters; for either he will hate the one and love the other, or he will be devoted to one and despise the other. You cannot serve God and wealth" (v. 24).

It seems as though Jesus was always asking, "What do you value most?" He was always contrasting two perspectives—for example, two kingdoms, two masters, or two values. So what do fit churches value most? Simply put, they value investing in heavenly wealth. The key question for fit churches is, "Where is our treasure?"

You might be a fit church if . . .

- You teach regularly on biblical stewardship of time, treasure, and talent.
- You have a systematic stewardship program.
- You are known for handling church resources wisely.
- You align your budget with the church's vision, values, and goals.

- You exercise faith when establishing the annual budget.
- You communicate expectations for all attendees to participate in regular giving.
- You require church leaders to be regular financial contributors in order to serve.

Handling Money

Money has two primary distinctions in the Bible. It can be an instrument of good or an instrument of evil, and God does not leave us in the dark about how we should manage it. Consider the following biblical guidelines for managing money, and think about what they mean for a church.

The spiritual condition of the giver is important (see Ps. 51:10, 17, 19).

If your riches increase, do not set your heart on them (see Ps. 62:10).

We must first seek God's kingdom and righteousness (see Matt. 6:33).

God's grace calls believers to be generous (see Acts 4:32–35).

We are to give to God on the first day of the week (see 1 Cor. 16:2).

Even the poor can be generous in giving (see 2 Cor. 8:1–2).

Giving is first to the Lord, but is also a way to serve others (see vv. 4–6).

Believers should excel in everything, including the grace of giving (see v. 7).

Financial giving is a test of our sacrificial love (see v. 8).

Leaders should train believers to give (see 2 Cor. 9:3–5).

Those who handle God's money wisely will receive more so that they may be even more generous (see vv. 10–14).

Leaders must be trustworthy with money (see 1 Tim. 3:2–3).

Accumulating money wrongly will bring harm (see James 5:1–3).

These passages present several principles that fit churches wisely embrace in their stewardship ministries.

Unfortunately, in many churches the lack of God-honoring stewardship is a major crisis, which, if allowed to continue without some intervention, will only get worse. In contrast to the lack of good financial stewardship found in some churches, fit churches honor God in the use of their finances. They believe wholeheartedly that to give is to sow, which results in generous churches. Writing to the Corinthians, Paul introduced an important piece of doctrinal instruction. "Now this I say," Paul begins, which is his way of saying "pay attention—this is important." "He who sows sparingly will also reap sparingly, and he who sows bountifully will also reap bountifully" (2 Cor. 9:6). While Paul was talking to individual believers, he addressed the church in Corinth as a whole body. Fit churches apply this passage to themselves in understanding that by being generous, the church is sowing seed. Like a farmer, leaders in fit churches recognize that when seed is sown, it may disappear for a time, but contrary to appearances, it will produce fruit in the future. Thus, fit churches seek to give generously to their staffs, their people, and the world around them, realizing that by doing so they will reap fruit in the future. The fruit reaped may be new believers or goodwill in the community or happy staff members.

Fit churches recognize their attitude toward finances reveals the heart of the congregation. Paul told the Corinthians, "Each one must do just as he has purposed in his heart, not grudgingly or under compulsion, for God loves a cheerful giver" (v. 7). Here Paul notes the quality of the gift is more important than the amount of the gift. The source of a church's generosity is not its budget but its heart. Churches that choose to hoard money rather than provide generously for their staff, programs, and community outreach reveal a miserly heart. Each church should cheerfully give to others, but the Lord doesn't have a specific quota or standard percentage he expects churches to provide. Like people, churches are free to control their expenditures as the leaders think best. Yet the true measure of a church's heart is seen in its attitude of generosity. Since church leaders expect members to be generous in giving to the church, should they not lead the church in generously investing its resources for others?

The leaders of fit churches also realize that as they model generosity, God will meet the church's financial needs and even provide additional income so they can sow even more in outreach ministries. "Now He who supplies seed to the sower and bread for food will supply and multiply your seed for sowing and increase the harvest of your righteousness; you will be enriched in everything for all liberality, which through us is producing thanksgiving to God" (vv. 10–11). As churches generously invest the finances God provides to serve others, he in turn provides even more income to meet their needs and presents more to invest. Being generous inspires thanksgiving to God. Generous churches literally enrich the corporate soul of the congregation while relieving others' pains, inspiring people to praise God.

Solid Stewardship Practices

Church leaders spend a great deal of time figuring out how to reduce spending but give little attention to increasing giving. Perhaps they get what they expect—low giving. Fit churches find the following practices help them increase giving so they can be generous.

First, fit churches work from a well-defined budget. As churches go through predictable economic ups and downs, leaders find it extremely helpful to work from a well-defined budget. Most often, I find church budgets are divided into six categories.

Salaries/benefits. This includes cash salaries for pastors and support staff, as well as a host of possible benefits, such as retirement contributions, medical insurance, tuition assistance, etc.

Missions. This includes financial support for foreign and home missionaries, which may be a percentage of the general church budget or raised through separate offerings.

Education/discipleship. This includes expenditures for study materials, school curriculum, and various other resources that assist in spiritual formation.

Mortgage/debt service. This includes all payments to pay off debt, usually for physical property.

Fixed operation costs. This includes all costs of doing business, such as insurance, upkeep, utilities, etc.

Evangelism/outreach. This includes money for outreach in the immediate community, including advertising, visitor welcome packets, training materials, etc.

Second, fit churches develop a ratio of expenditures to various operations and adjust it from year to year. Obviously, ratios of expenditures to operations vary from church to church. The size, age, location, complexity, and demographic profile of a church make setting standard guidelines difficult, but the following are typical guidelines employed by fit churches.

Salaries/benefits. Churches usually spend between a high of 89 percent and a low of 27 percent of the total church budget on salaries and benefits. Smaller churches tend to dedicate a higher percentage and larger churches a lower percentage.

Missions. The rule that many churches use for giving to foreign and home missions is a tithe (10 percent) of the total church budget. Some churches raise money for missions through special offerings and give between 15 and 20 percent. A few churches dedicate 50 percent of their budgets to missions but create problems funding local ministry by doing so.

Education/discipleship. Expenses for spiritual formation are normally about 10 percent of the church budget. This may be higher in churches with large, traditional Sunday school programs but can be lower in churches that use small groups.

Mortgage/debt service. This category of expenditures has the potential to strap a church's ministry if it is too high. It is best if the cost of debt service does not take more than 15 percent of the total church budget, but in today's economy, 25 percent is not an unusual percentage. If the amount of a church's budget rises above 25 percent, the church's ministry is often hampered because funds are taken away that could be used for more direct ministry.

Fixed operation costs. Fixed costs are expenses that do not change much over time, such as rent, utilities, and insurance. Other expenses that may change yearly are called variable costs. It is best if a church's fixed costs are in the range of 15 percent of the budget, but this varies greatly according to the location of the church.

Evangelism/outreach. The amount dedicated for evangelism and outreach usually represents the lowest percentage of a church's budget expenditures. This is unfortunate, since money spent in this category is the most likely to bring new people to Christ and the church. Growing churches typically spend a minimum of 5 percent of the entire church budget for evangelism and outreach. The fastest-growing churches target up to 10 percent of the budget for this category.

Third, fit churches place a priority on staff, ministry, and facilities—in that order. While each church allocates budget expenditures differently, wise leaders make staffing a priority. In many ways, the quality of the staff determines the future of the church. Fit churches typically spend between 40 and 50 percent of their budgets on staff salaries, benefits, and reimbursements. While some churches proudly declare they give 50 percent of every dollar to missions, there is usually an unseen problem— the staff members are not generously paid. In other words, to give half of its income to missions, a church usually does so to the neglect of its own staff, which is certainly unbiblical. Fit churches follow the lead of Scripture, which declares, "The one who is taught the word is to share all good things with the one who teaches" (Gal. 6:6). "The elders who rule well are to be considered worthy of double honor, especially those who work hard at preaching and teaching. For the Scripture says, 'YOU SHALL NOT MUZZLE THE OX WHILE HE IS THRESHING,' and 'The laborer is worthy of his wages'" (1 Tim. 5:17–18).

Fourth, fit churches plan for funding God's work. Nehemiah is one example of a leader who understood stewardship principles. After learning the walls of Jerusalem were in ruins, he prayed about it (see Neh. 1:4–11). The fact that he spent time praying about the issue before designing his plan points to the purity of his motives. During Nehemiah's prayer, God revealed to him a mission to rebuild the walls. Fit church leaders realize the truth that people give to vision, and they work hard to find and communicate a clear vision for the future of the church they lead.

Nehemiah asked directly for what he needed to complete God's vision (see 2:4–8). He developed a plan, knew what resources were needed, and asked the right person to help. Of course, Nehemiah understood the resources were God's, but he was ready when the king asked him to give a specific, detailed response regarding what was needed. The leaders of fit churches understand they must do the work of developing plans and guiding God's people to give sacrificially to accomplish God's plans in the world.

Fifth, fit churches train their people to give. In many churches today, very few people appear to give from the firstfruits of their income, with church members giving only about 2–3 percent of their income to their church, while living on the remaining 97–98 percent. Ten percent of people give 75 percent of the total income of the church, with only 25 percent of the church's total income coming from the remaining 90 percent of the people. Less than 20 percent of churches teach worshipers to give financially. Oftentimes pressure tactics, budget appeals, garage sales, legalistic petitions, and additional strategies influence people's financial giving. While these often produce a short-term response, it is far better to teach people to follow biblical principles. Giving flows most naturally from an informed mind and a loving heart. Waldo Werning, former director of the Discipling/Stewardship Center in Fort Wayne, Indiana, writes, "We cannot expect fiscal responsibility from people whose belief system is weakened by a crisis of faith. The best predictor of generous giving is a strong faith and an informed mind. To be a faithful steward, a Christian must be fed and in a healthy congregation."[1]

Sixth, fit churches prepare a resource development strategy. A good plan includes a specific strategy to communicate the vision, needs, and opportunities for giving all year long. Such a strategy involves an annual stewardship emphasis, instruction on giving in new member classes, biblical teaching on giving each year from the pulpit, personal testimonies from those who give, annual commitment cards, specific giving projects, and regular reporting on the church's finances to the total constituency.

Fit churches build trust with the congregation by taking care of financial business and by how church leaders spend the church's money. Leaders must spend wisely. When church attendees see they can trust their leaders not to overspend, and thus get maximum value out of the budget, they become more generous in their giving. Proper accounting of income and expenditures is also essential. Fit churches insist on proper accountability and organize the financial affairs of the church to keep risks at a minimum. Churches are not immune from dishonesty and temptation in financial affairs. Establishing controls to help eliminate problems builds trust among the people. This means separating roles; for example, the person who writes checks should not deposit money. A yearly audit by an independent, qualified outside firm also builds trust. Requiring detailed reports from the treasurer is also a critical component. Monitoring the cash flow, accounts payable, budget percentages, and legitimacy of expenses week to week pays off. Such actions keep the church on track financially and may save the church thousands of dollars.

Trust also comes from being able to raise money for the church and its special projects. Along with having godly character, which is the primary requirement, potential board members must also bring qualifications of wisdom, work, and wealth, but too often we overlook the importance of understanding wealth and settle for too many people who just bring wisdom and work to a board. While board members do not need to be wealthy, a key part of board leadership is assuming primary responsibility for securing financial resources. When church leaders are able to handle money wisely and help raise the level of financial giving, they prove themselves as leaders and find the congregation will quickly rally behind their vision and goals.

Five Types of Churches

Beginner Churches

Beginner churches haphazardly handle their financial affairs. A single person or members of the same family control accounting functions. Teaching on the subject of financial stewardship rarely occurs from the pulpit or in classes or small groups. Beginner churches have no organized stewardship plan in place. Urgent financial appeals are regularly given in emergency situations or at the end of the church's fiscal year. The financial books are cared for by a church volunteer, who may keep the books and records at their home.

PLAN OF ACTION IF YOU LEAD A BEGINNER CHURCH

- Encourage the pastor to preach or teach a series on biblical stewardship in the coming year.
- Evaluate who handles money in the church and separate the functions of counting, depositing, approving expenditures, and writing checks among four different people and/or families in the church.
- If your church does not operate with a yearly budget, develop a budget for the coming year and track income and expenditures.
- Require that all financial books and records remain at the church office rather than in the home of a volunteer treasurer or accountant.
- Give a minimum of 10 percent of your church's income to international missions.

Novice Churches

Novice churches have basic budgets in place, and leaders receive monthly reports on income, expenditures, accounts payable, and projections for the rest of the year. The churches implement financial stewardship campaigns once a year, during which time people are encouraged to give sacrificially to ministries. Special offerings for a few specific projects are taken during the year.

Plan of Action If You Lead a Novice Church

- Move away from a volunteer treasurer or accountant as soon as possible by hiring a part-time employee or contracting with an outside firm to take care of the financial records.
- Complete a ministry audit of where money is invested, and evaluate the value of each investment. For example, how much money is being spent on worship, administration, care ministry, education/small groups, children's ministry, youth ministry, facilities, etc.
- To get a larger picture of the cost of each ministry category, place a portion of each staff member's salary into each category of ministry. For example, if the pastor spends 50 percent of his time on worship, 30 percent of his time on administration, and 20 percent of his time on pastoral care, then dedicate 50 percent of his salary to the worship category, 30 percent to administration, and 20 percent to care ministry. Do this with each staff member to obtain an accurate picture of the real cost of each area of ministry or service. Then evaluate the true investment costs and return to the total ministry. Where are the largest costs? Where are the greatest returns? How does this fit with the church's mission, vision, and goals?
- Give 10 percent of the budget to international missions and 5 percent to outreach in the church's immediate ministry area.
- Put enough money in reserve for three months' worth of expenses.

Intermediate Churches

Intermediate churches have part-time paid treasurers and/or accountants who do the books on-site. An independent, outside firm conducts a yearly audit to assure good accountability.

PLAN OF ACTION IF YOU LEAD AN INTERMEDIATE CHURCH

- Determine the major financial categories of the budget and develop expected percentages for each area.
- Hire a full-time treasurer or accountant as soon as possible.
- Develop a detailed financial stewardship plan for the entire church year.
- Save a four-month reserve of money to be used in emergencies or during times of financial downturn.
- Give 10 percent of the budget to international missions, 5 percent to outreach in the church's immediate ministry area, and 5 percent to church planting.

Advanced Churches

Advanced churches staff full-time accountants who handle the financial books in a highly professional manner. Weekly reports on income, expenditures, accounts payable, and future projects are on the pastor's desk each week. The church develops a budget each year with the input of every ministry leader.

PLAN OF ACTION IF YOU LEAD AN ADVANCED CHURCH

- Put aside enough cash to cover five months' worth of expenses.
- Invest in a pastor of outreach and assimilation.
- Raise money to support a church planter and start a daughter church.

- Investigate how other churches the same size engage their people in active stewardship.
- Hire a professional accountant on the church staff.

Elite Churches

Elite churches employ specialists to take excellent care of the church's finances. A well-respected, independent firm conducts a yearly audit with no conflict of interest to the church. Due to many years of excellent stewardship training, the people give sacrificially to the general budget, as well as to several special projects.

PLAN OF ACTION IF YOU LEAD AN ELITE CHURCH

- Keep enough cash in reserve to cover six months' worth of expenses.
- Increase the level of monitoring of church finances, especially the oversight of those who handle the weekly offerings, deposits, and expenditure of funds.
- Bring in an outside consulting firm to analyze the church's total financial stewardship process and plan.
- Invest in a church multiplication pastor and help plant a church every two years.
- Openly report the church's financial condition to all its constituents.

Main Points

- *Beginner church*: displays limited financial accountability and stewardship teaching.
- *Novice church*: has basic budget systems in place.
- *Intermediate church*: demonstrates increased stewardship and financial rigor.
- *Advanced church*: shifts percentage of finances toward missional activity.
- *Elite church*: sacrificial giving is in the church's DNA.

LEADERSHIP DEVELOPMENT

Leadership is a team sport. You cannot effectively lead solo or in a vacuum. You need to be committed to developing other leaders. Leadership has little to do with followers and much more to do with developing other leaders. Leadership expert John Maxwell says, "If you really want to be a successful leader, you must develop the leaders around you."[1] I have found that leaders want to be successful. So what can you do to develop other leaders in your church?

Leadership development must involve leader-development capacity, a culture of leadership development, and a leadership development pipeline.

Determine Your Leader-Development Capacity

Growth is more than a hobby; it is a habit. The person who chooses to be a leader developer must work at integrating the nine qualities below into their life.

You might be a fit church if . . .

- You have identified those gifted and called to leadership.
- You actively recruit and assess qualified people for leadership roles.
- You welcome new leaders within the congregation.
- You formally evaluate the performance of all leaders each year.

- You recognize and honor people for their effective leadership.
- You trust your leaders and actively follow them.
- You hold your leaders accountable for clearly defined expectations.

A leader developer appreciates others. Authentic appreciation is the primary motivator for development. When people know you appreciate them for who they are, they are more open to development. Appreciating people where they are and as they are puts you in a position to begin the development process. Appreciation means acknowledging a person's strengths, abilities, and skills. Once you have done this, you can hone who they are.

A leader developer believes in the propensity of others to do their best. Leadership development is not a journey of imagination; it is an adventure of building up people who you believe want to do the work. If you question a person's desire, you will limit your investment in them. So if you do not believe they will do their best, then do not invest in them.

A leader developer praises people for what they have done. Accomplishment is the fruit of development. What receives recognition is what gets accomplished. If you do not applaud (praise) what someone does, then they will soon stop doing it. A person knows they are developing when they accomplish milestones you have laid out in the development process. Unpraised steps will soon result in standing still.

A *leader developer empowers others.* They understand the positive process of allowing people to learn through failure. Empowerment allows for this. Followers are given the space and freedom to try. Their development is enhanced when, after they try, there is debriefing. Debriefing moves experience into acquired wisdom.

A *leader developer listens and asks questions.* They first listen, then probe through questions. It's important to allow the person being developed to be heard. The leader developer gains a better understanding of the other person's perspectives and intentions when they listen to them. Once the person being developed has been heard, the leader developer can use questions as leverage points to help the person think for themselves.

A *leader developer encourages and cares for others.* They deeply understand the power of encouragement and care in developing other people. Offering encouragement and care pushes folks to the next level of growth. The leader developer can challenge the status quo, cultivate an environment of trust, and change the thinking of the person being developed from "no way" to "what is the best way."

A *leader developer values clear thinking and strategic action.* They are intentional. They lay out a path to develop others. They refuse to take a happenstance approach. They are willing to adapt the developmental process but not at the expense of the end result.

A *leader developer continually learns and places a high value on personal growth.* They know they are on a journey of growth. They are intimately aware that their willingness to grow, learn, and develop feeds directly into their ability to develop others. Being a lifelong learner is essential for a leader developer.

A leader developer accepts personal responsibility to develop others. They embrace this responsibility. They understand that you get who you develop. Where you invest your time is where you will reap your greatest benefit.

How do you measure up to these nine qualities? What can you do to integrate them into your role as a leader developer? What will you do? When will you do this?

Establish a Culture of Leader Development

One thing Phil most looked forward to when moving into high school was the opportunity to play organized football. The football program had three levels: freshman, junior varsity, and varsity. The freshman team was only for those in their freshman year. Therefore, it was age-driven. The other two levels were primarily skill-based.

The ultimate goal was for players at the varsity level to be skilled and to understand both the offensive and defensive systems. The methodology used to facilitate this was age-appropriate development and shared understanding.

Beginning at the freshman level, coaches taught the skill sets needed at the varsity level. Along with skill development, the same offensive and defensive systems used at the varsity level were implemented. This resulted in a culture of shared values, skills, and systems. The ultimate result was winning football games.

Leadership is needed at every level of a church that chooses to run the race well. A church that builds a culture that prioritizes developing leaders will exponentially increase its effectiveness. So what can a church do to build a leadership culture?

The pastor must be convinced that a leadership culture is necessary. Many pastors prefer to hold tight to the leaders already in place. Such an attitude will eventually stagnate a church. However, when a pastor is genuinely convinced that new leaders need to be developed throughout the ranks, the culture is primed for change.

Assuming you support the necessity of building a leadership culture, you can do some things to construct your framework. And, like Phil's high school football program, you must begin at the lowest level.

First, define leadership. John Maxwell says, "Leadership is not about titles, positions, flowcharts. It is about one life influencing another."[2] This definition reveals the importance of building a leadership culture. People will influence others, so you want them to influence well. Whatever your definition, make it clear, concise, and communicable. How do you define leadership?

Second, view every person as a potential leader. The lenses through which you view others will greatly determine your interaction with them. Seeing every person as a potential leader will help you view them differently. You will observe the little things they do. You will note how they relate to others. You will consider how they handle challenges. Viewing others as potential leaders will enhance your ability to zero in on their leadership capacity. How do you view those in your congregation?

Third, identify core leadership competencies. Competencies are the skills needed to lead in your congregation. A leadership culture is built on shared competencies. All leaders need the following basic competencies: problem-solving skills, the ability to connect relationally, and the knack for communicating well. Additionally, each church has its own unique competencies.

Several years ago, Phil determined to establish a process for developing emerging leaders in the district he oversaw. He reflected back on his experiences and identified nine core ministry competencies and established a question to evaluate the competence in each of the areas.

Nine Core Competencies	Questions to Evaluate Competence
Spiritual Disciplines	How do I consistently connect with God?
Self-Leadership	What systems of accountability do I currently practice?
Serving Others	Who do I serve or help for no personal gain?
Leadership Style	How do I live out my unique leadership abilities?
Relating to Others	How do I build and maintain healthy relationships?
Communication	How do I improve my communication skills?
Lifelong Learning	What personal development plan do I currently employ?
Developing Leaders	How do I currently develop leaders?
Growing and Multiplying Ministry	How do I multiply myself and my ministry?

Phil established these for his particular area of ministry responsibility. We provide them as an example, not with the expectation that they will be yours. Instead, think about what core leadership competencies are needed in your church.

Fourth, develop a process to coach people in the core competencies. We use the word *coach*, as opposed to *train*, intentionally. Training is content-based, while coaching is relationally based. Coaching people in the core competencies puts them in relational connections for mentoring and maturing in leadership. A coach is one who comes alongside a potential leader to help them discover their leadership capacity. Here are eight ways to maximize leadership development through coaching.

> *Connect relationally.* You impact people from a distance, but you influence them up close. You will never effectively develop leaders from afar. Connecting is about being *with* people not merely *around* them. You can be around people without being with them, but you cannot be with them

unless you are around them. Get around and with those you are developing. Invest in them. Let them see your life.

Open doors to experiences. Experiences are things you do and involve people you meet. You can share a variety of experiences with those you are developing. Experiences can be locations, activities, or challenges. They are anything you might provide to those you are developing that will enlarge their horizons and increase their opportunities. The key, however, is not simply to experience but to debrief the experience.

> You impact people from a distance, but you influence them up close.

Ask open-ended questions. Leaders need to be taught *how* to think, not *what* to think. Open-ended questions empower this development. "The heart of coaching is simple: you can help people significantly by listening and asking good questions."[3] The questions force developing leaders to think, apply, probe, and decide. They own the choices they make.

Capture their hearts. People you are developing buy into you before they buy into the mission. You capture their hearts when you give them your heart (the authentic you) and your hand (help in their lives). You capture their hearts when you believe in their potential and who they are as human beings. You capture their hearts when you add value to their lives.

Hold them accountable. Accountability must be agreed on. It is ineffective if only one person agrees on the areas of accountability. Leaders who are not held accountable for their attitudes, actions, and abilities are being shortchanged in their development.

Invite them to fail. You and leaders you are developing must view failure as an opportunity to learn. Failure is only final if you never fail again; and the only time you will never fail is if you stop trying. Never allow those you are developing to stop trying.

Utilize need-oriented resourcing. Give developing leaders what they need, not what they want. Delve into your experiential toolbox and supply them with resources you know they will need. John Wooden, legendary University of California, Los Angeles, basketball coach, spent the first practice of every basketball season teaching his players how to put on their socks and tie their shoes. Why? The players did not want or value such mundane information, but Wooden knew they needed it. Ill-fitting socks and recklessly tied shoes could result in blisters. And blisters could keep them from giving their best when their best was needed.

Give them honest feedback. Speak the truth in love. Be clear. Be kind. Be gentle.

How are you developing leaders in your congregation? What coaching skills do you need to develop to increase your capacity to develop leaders?

Fifth, put people in the process. A process does no good if you are not placing people in it. Create a method for people in your church to enter the leadership development process. The first step is to identify individuals who may be candidates. I suggest three characteristics to look for in potential leaders.

Honesty. A leader understands the value of honesty. A leader hones their ability to speak in a forthright but fair manner. The Bible describes this as the leader who will "speak the truth in love" (Eph. 4:15 NLT). An honest leader does not have to belittle, speak down to, degrade, or demoralize others. An honest leader does not have to spin reality, sugarcoat situations, or comment on circumstances overly optimistically. An honest leader speaks their mind. They are clear in their communication. They state the situation in the proper context, using well-chosen words, and consider the emotions of others.

Passion. When a leader believes in something, they pursue it with controlled abandon. They are not afraid of pouring themselves into the mission, goal, or dream. Passion compels others. Passion attracts others. Passion fuels individuals and churches. Passion propels a leader's pursuit. And a leader's pursuit increases their passion. A leader should not back down from what they are passionate about.

Risk-taking. Challenges are risky. When a leader accepts a challenge, it is inherent with risk. They may risk their reputation, competency, credibility, fortune, or dream.

When you view these three characteristics in someone, they have the potential to be developed as a leader. How are you identifying potential leaders? How are you getting people into the developmental process?

Sixth, build in multiplication. A leadership culture *must* have multiplication built into it. People should not only be developed but also be developing others. Developed leaders who are not developing other leaders are limited to one generation of leaders. Genuine leadership development has not occurred until a leader has multiplied other leaders. If you are not multiplying leaders, then you are developing followers, not leaders. What are you doing to multiply generations of leaders?

Building a leadership culture is time-intensive but cost-effective. A church that builds leadership into its culture will never be static. People will grow. Ministry will be valued. Communities will be influenced. Your church will run the race effectively!

Create a Leadership Development Pipeline

Leaders do not merely accumulate followers; they activate other leaders. John Maxwell states, "My goal is not to draw a following that results in a crowd. My goal is to develop leaders who become a movement."[4] A leader who does not take this to heart will have limited leadership effectiveness. A leader who resists developing other leaders will have limited influence during their life span. A leader who genuinely desires a life of significance will develop the leaders who will outlive them.

Business leader Kent Humphreys owned and operated a national general merchandise distribution company. During his tenure as a business owner, he discovered the importance of developing other leaders. In his wonderful book *Shepherding Horses*,[5] Kent outlines six steps for raising up and training leaders.

Step 1: Invite them to join you. Developing leaders begins with an invite for them to participate with you. Leaders seldom respond to a general call to be developed. But when they are asked specifically, they have a tendency to be more open to participating. Invite those you want to develop into a vibrant relationship of growth with you.

Step 2: Create a trust-filled atmosphere. It is difficult to develop leaders in distrust. Those you are developing must trust you. You build trust through patience, transparency, and modeling.

Step 3: Affirm their potential. Many of those you choose to develop may not see in themselves what you see in them. Let them know why you believe in them. Show them their potential. Be specific in your affirmation. When they do not believe in themselves, you believe in them!

Step 4: Give them practical skills. Because competency is a necessary skill for doing the work of a leader, it is a key element of leadership development. Other key skills include relationship building, organization, communication, and strategic implementation.

Step 5: Confirm their leadership. Be public about your developmental process. Those you are developing need your blessing. Place the mantle on them. Be clear about your expectations. Confirm them in their role now and in the future.

Step 6: Release them to lead. Developing leaders but never releasing them to lead will frustrate them. An unwillingness to release others will undermine you. If you become known as a developer who does not release, you will have a difficult time recruiting others to join you on future leadership developmental journeys. Leadership development goes beyond training and coaching and into the opportunity to implement the training.

Leaders are developers. They develop people to become leaders. Developing leaders is the key to creating synergy and movement in the leadership capacity of the local church. How are you moving followers into leaders? Who are you developing as a leader? Designing a process to develop present and future leaders is a critical component of building the body.

Five Types of Churches

Beginner Churches

Beginner churches rely solely on the pastor for everything related to leadership. The pastor leads everything, initiates most things, and often is the only person willing to head committees or teams. The few who are willing to chair a committee or team are typically not leaders. They act in this role only to appease the pastor. The same folks serve in the same roles for long periods of time because no other leaders are being developed. The pastor seldom has much confidence in their leadership capabilities.

Plan of Action If You Lead a Beginner Church

- Develop a personal plan to read three books on leadership.
- Encourage the pastor to attend one leadership-intensive seminar or conference.
- Make a list of at least three people you view as potential leaders.

Novice Churches

Novice churches have begun to sense the need for leadership development within their churches. The pastor of a novice church has gotten to the point where he is unwilling to lead everything. The local church board has begun to sense the limitation of their leadership capacity. This realization is the agitation needed to begin to move forward.

Plan of Action If You Lead a Novice Church

- Have the board read and discuss one leadership book a year.
- Encourage the pastor or a designated key lay leader to lead a discussion each month with the board about insights found in their reading.
- Encourage the pastor to preach a sermon series on biblical leadership principles.
- Provide training for your church's second-tier leaders (small group leaders, teachers, and ministry leaders) in basic leadership concepts.

Intermediate Churches

Intermediate churches have leadership boards that are growing in their leadership capacity. The pastors and boards of intermediate churches are learning more of what it means to lead. Leadership lessons and conversations about application are a central aspect of each board meeting. Board meetings are more about looking ahead than managing property and handling crises.

PLAN OF ACTION IF YOU LEAD AN INTERMEDIATE CHURCH

- The pastor selects a group of folks (three to six people) from the congregation he believes have leadership potential.
- He extends an invitation for this group to join him on a leadership development journey.
- He selects one of the books he has read and the board has discussed for everyone in the group to read.
- The group meets regularly, and the pastor asks good questions.
- The board members identify others they would like to participate in another leadership development group, perhaps led by the pastor.

Advanced Churches

Advanced churches are highly engaged in leadership development. The local board members are leading leadership development groups. The pastors are beginning new leadership development groups on a regular basis. Each person who participates in a leadership development group is expected to multiply this in others. A *farm system* of new leaders is being developed. Those who lead ministry teams/committees are expected to be developing other leaders.

Plan of Action If You Lead an Advanced Church

The following steps should be taken by the lead pastor or a person designated by the pastor.

- Develop a list of leadership skills and competencies central to all leaders in the congregation.
- Design a plan to teach these competencies. The plan should include books and lessons for discussion and interaction.
- Select leaders to participate in this deeper leadership development process.
- Test drive the process and evaluate.
- Hold quarterly leadership gatherings for all ministry leaders.

Elite Churches

Elite churches have leadership development happening at every level of their congregations. The expectation for leadership development is part of the fabric of these churches. And people are attracted to them because of this leadership culture. High-capacity leaders are the new normal. Leadership pipelines are in place. Leaders are raised up not only for each church's ministry but also to be sent out to other ministries. The local leadership boards and other ministry departments have a continual infusion of new leadership blood.

Plan of Action If You Lead an Elite Church

- Expose the congregation to outside leadership experts.
- Make the growth of the leadership pipeline a key metric in ministry effectiveness.
- Take potential leaders to a leadership conference each year.
- Resist leadership complacency.

Churches that are building the body value leadership development. They recognize that developing new leaders increases the capacity and competency of the church. A church that intentionally works to develop leaders, both present and future, increases its *muscular strength* to face the future.

Main Points

- *Beginner church*: recycles leaders.
- *Novice church*: recognizes its leadership limitations.
- *Intermediate church*: begins to expose the local church board to leadership development.
- *Advanced church*: people are meeting in groups for leadership development.
- *Elite church*: leaders are being multiplied and sent out.

PART 3

Muscular Endurance

Muscular endurance is closely aligned with muscular strength. While muscular strength deals with exertion in a single effort, muscular endurance relates to doing something repeatedly. As we highlighted earlier, muscular endurance is the ability of a muscle or group of muscles to repeatedly exert force against resistance. The characteristics that provide for muscular endurance are Christ-exalting worship, disciple-making strategy, and pastoral leadership. These characteristics provide the needed strength to continue for the long haul.

7

CHRIST-EXALTING WORSHIP

Call it exalting, inspiring, celebrative, stimulating, encouraging, rousing, engaging, moving, energizing, or whatever other adjective you desire, worship is a major sign of a fit church. Respected researcher Kirk Hadaway explains:

> Worship in growing churches, and especially in rapidly growing churches, has a different character from worship in plateaued and declining congregations. This character is somewhat difficult to describe, but the terms usually employed are "excitement," "celebration," "electricity," and "spirit of revival." Whatever terms are used, anyone who has worshipped in many growing congregations will agree that the worship experience sets these churches apart.[1]

Former pastor Dale Galloway agrees. "Worship is a wonderful marvelous mystery," he writes. "Nothing in this world is greater than to be in a service where your spirit meets with God's spirit. That is the high moment in the community of the church."[2]

When corporate worship inspires, people come to the service expecting God to work, sinners to repent, the sick to be made whole, the hurting to be restored, and the Word of God preached

> **You might be a fit church if you . . .**
> - Insist on excellence in worship.
> - Plan your worship services six months in advance.
> - Evaluate your past worship services each week.
> - Use a variety of music.
> - Pace the worship service to fit today's culture.
> - Engage people in active service to God.
> - Encourage people to respect God's work.

in such a manner that people are challenged to live life with vibrancy and to take appropriate action in the world.

What Is Worship?

Have you ever noticed how we casually use the word *worship* without really considering its meaning? Listen around church this next weekend and you will hear people say, "I'm going to *worship*" or "Where is the *worship* center?" or "Did you enjoy *worship* today?" We once overheard one person say, "I listened to the *worship* leader and the *worship* team sing *worship* songs." Worship is a familiar word, but how often do we really think about what it means? What is worship?

The Bible provides two essential pillars with which to understand worship. First, worship is an expression of respect and submission. The main Hebrew word in the Old Testament is *shahah*, which is translated "to bow down." Such an expression is most often seen in the physical act of bowing down, kneeling, or prostrating oneself to another person. For example, when the people of Israel heard of God's concern for them from Moses and Aaron, "they *bowed low and worshiped*" (Exod. 4:31, emphasis added). Solomon writes concerning the nomads and kings of the earth, "May he also rule from sea to sea and from the River to the ends of the earth. Let the nomads of the desert *bow before him*, and his enemies lick the dust. Let the kings of Tarshish and of the islands bring presents; the kings of Sheba and Seba offer gifts. And let all kings *bow down before him*, all nations serve him" (Ps. 72:8–11, emphasis added). The New Testament word for worship is *proskuneo*, and it echoes the image of worship in the Old Testament. It is a combination of *pros*, meaning "toward," and *kuneo*, meaning "to kiss," which creates a clear image of one bowing low to kiss the hand or feet of another person. Thus, the first pillar of worship is to show respect and submission to another.

Second, worship is an act of sacrifice and obedience, which normally is seen in service to God. For example, the psalmist writes, "This will be written for the generation to come, that a people yet to be created may praise the Lord. . . . When the peoples are gathered together, and the kingdoms, *to serve* the Lord" (Ps. 102:18, 22, emphasis added). The word used in the Old Testament is *asab*, meaning "to carve, labor, or to serve." In the New Testament, the word is *latreuo*, which means "to serve." It is the word from which we get liturgy, which essentially means a service to the Lord. Thus, the second pillar of worship is any act of sacrificial service done for the Lord. To worship is a response from our hearts to God for what he has done and who he is eternally. Such a response is actively seen in our respectful submission and active obedience to God.

Characteristics of Worship

Music and worship go together. Historically the actual practice of worship has varied greatly. In the Middle Ages, the use of Gregorian Chant, which was monophonic (unison singing), a capella (no use of instruments), and nonmetrical (no accents), was common (e.g., "O Come, O Come, Immanuel"). Following the Protestant Reformation in 1517, the hymns and chorales of Luther (e.g., "A Mighty Fortress Is Our God") became popular. Then in the 1700s, Isaac Watts, the father of English hymnody, began paraphrasing the biblical text, particularly the Psalms (e.g., "O God, Our Help in Ages Past," which is based on Psalm 90). Around the same time, Johann Sebastian Bach wrote numerous chorales for Lutheran church worship (e.g., "Jesu, Joy of Man's Desiring"). As the Great Awakening of the mid- to late 1700s arose, John and Charles Wesley introduced hymns of invitation (e.g., "And Can It Be That I Should Gain") that spoke to the audience of their day.

In the Americas of the 1800s, folk melodies were merged with classic hymnody to create gospel songs that were used in the more informal personal worship environments of the Baptist and Methodist Camp Meetings. During this time, the gospel songs of Fanny Crosby were quite popular (e.g., "I Am Thine, O Lord"). She began a style of Christian singing that stressed our personal relationship with God rather than his attributes and character. The popularity of gospel singing was propelled into the early 1900s through the revivals of preacher-musician teams, such as Dwight L. Moody and Ira D. Sankey (late 1800s), Billy Sunday and Homer Rodeheaver (1900–1930), and Billy Graham and Cliff Barrows (1945–2005). Christian music of the mid-1900s continued this tradition through the easily sung music of John W. Peterson (1950–1970; e.g., "It Took a Miracle") and Bill and Gloria Gaither (1960s to the early 2000s; e.g., "The King Is Coming"). Beginning in the mid-1960s, the Jesus Movement created big changes in church music, from a reliance on large choirs supported by piano and organ to the use of small worship teams supported by guitars and drums. Contemporary music was institutionalized through the popularity of the larger megachurches and the formation of the Christian music industry.

Today Christian worship continues to undergo significant changes. Like it or not, television and the internet set the expected standards for communication among today's younger generations. People make value judgments quickly since they have many choices from which to select. Entertainment has raised the expectations so high that many church worship services appear mediocre in comparison. Today's younger generations no longer tolerate haphazardly planned worship services. They do not have their grandparents' or parents' sense of duty to continue to support a worship service that no longer connects with their issues and needs. They value an authentic experience that includes some level of involvement, whether it is handclapping, hand-raising, or quiet meditation in a dark worship center. Formality seems unnatural, as many participants feel it lacks genuineness. Thus, people usually seek informality, along with a relaxed atmosphere that doesn't pressure or seek to manipulate. Most, however, still prefer simple songs that express love and devotion while being built around solid doctrinal themes.

People's taste in music varies greatly, but it largely connects culturally with the worshipers. Generally, fit churches tend to have music that is celebrative and encouraging. A key ingredient of fit churches is a well-planned and executed worship service that involves people. While some worship services attract younger people due to the appearance of rough authenticity (often seen in the appropriately scruffy appearance of the worship band members), over the long-term, lack of planning does not hold people's attention. Worship has to be genuine—not just amusing. Bad worship is just bad, no matter the style. Some people are tempted to write off these expectations, calling some protestant worship simply talent shows.[3] However, doing things well is not just entertainment, as the late Robert Webber, who wrote extensively on biblical worship, explains: "The church is to be a worshipping community *par excellence*, called to join the heavenly throng."[4]

Music Pastor to Worship Arts Pastor

Churches used to think in terms of a music pastor who exclusively focused on working with music in the church. Pastors had music degrees and expertise to lead choirs and orchestras. They were specialists in music. Gradually, a number of churches discovered what they really needed was a worship pastor, a person who could lead a congregation of people in public worship. Now churches seek a worship arts pastor to oversee a much broader range of ministry technology, visual arts, drama, dance, banners, etc.

One Style to Multiple Styles

Historically most churches offered one worship service in one style. Gradually churches started offering two worship services, but most still offered one style. As time went along, churches began offering multiple worship services and multiple styles in an attempt to reach new audiences for Christ. While some churches maintained at least one traditional worship service, each new style became increasingly contemporary or was perhaps in a different language. Generational issues played a major role in creating new forms of worship, as churches attempted to keep hold of their younger members.

Individuals to Team

For many years, worship involved star performers. Churches hired people to play the piano or organ or to sing special numbers. Now churches use teams to lead worship—sometimes multiple teams. Today many worship pastors are asked not whether they can lead worship (or music) but whether they can build teams.

Larger to Smaller

Large choirs and orchestras have been replaced in numerous churches by smaller worship teams and bands. The man-hour expense of large choirs kept too many people out of ministry opportunities. The same number of people may be involved in worship but most often gather in smaller groups of worship teams.

Big Event to Regular Event

Larger concerts, plays, and music programs used to draw in hundreds of newcomers to a church. However, the availability of many other types of events, e.g., Christian concerts, caused attendance at many local church events to go down. Today churches put more money into the weekly worship experiences. Events, of course, continue but are targeted more toward the unchurched than the already churched.

Preaching to Worship

Churches used to build worship spaces with little thought to the total worship experience. Most churches focused on highlighting the preaching and/or sacrament and ordinances. Today churches build worship auditoriums with staging, sound, lighting, and projection in mind. Churches that use different forms of art are specially designed to allow the art to share the stage.

Congregational Singing to Music Performance

Song leaders of past years did their best to get the congregation singing. People were encouraged to engage in worship by singing (even if their voices were not that good). Today many worshipers no longer participate through singing but rather engage in worship as part of an audience sharing a concert experience. There is danger in this, as true worship is participatory. "The difference between the church and the theater or the lecture hall is radical and must be expressed radically. The 'audience' in a church is God, and the people are all players, and they should all have a sense of being enmeshed in the action."[5]

These are just a few of the changes taking place in worship today. Each presents opportunities and challenges for anyone designing worship. Yet the call remains to develop worship services that inspire worshipers to respectfully submit to God and actively engage in service for God. Whatever style or approach you adopt for worship in your church, dynamic worship often has the following characteristics.

First, Christ-exalting worship is developed by a worship team rather than a single person. Worship teams are organized using three divisions: creative team, administrative team, and production team. The creative team develops, plans, and designs the worship services. The administrative team communicates between the team members and the congregation, researches new music, and oversees rehearsals, practice, writing, and arranging. The production team takes care of sound, lighting, tech, and setup. Together the team develops worship services that lift God up and draw worshipers to honor God.

Second, Christ-exalting worship is evaluated. A commitment to Christ-exalting worship involves regular study of the response of the congregation to worship services. If biblical worship is a valuable goal, then it is worth evaluating. Each week the worship team analyzes the successes and failures of the last worship service. The worship team asks questions, such as "What worked well?" "What didn't go well?" and "What could we do better?" The answers are discussed and evaluated with an attitude and expectation of continual improvement in future worship services.

Third, Christ-exalting worship is planned in advance. Worship teams dedicate a lot of creative thought to planning worship services ahead of time rather than haphazardly throwing them together at the last minute. Pastors plan their preaching calendars from three months to a year in advance, which allows worship leaders and teams to plan ahead for specific themes and topics. Services incorporate creative ideas and are organized two to three months in advance so participants can adequately practice, rehearse, and prepare for dynamic worship.

Fourth, Christ-exalting worship intentionally uses all areas of commendation. Worship teams acknowledge that worship is more than just mental agreement; it includes spiritual, relational, and emotional aspects. They therefore think about how to intentionally connect with worshipers in spiritual ways (e.g., prayer, quietness, lighting, etc.); mental ways (e.g., note sheets, visual tech, thought-provoking images, etc.); relational ways (e.g., speaking to others, shaking hands, clapping, etc.); and emotional ways (e.g., uplifted hands, kneeling, visual arts, etc.).

Fifth, Christ-exalting worship pays attention to the following six things: *pace* (Does the service move fast enough to hold people's attention?); *flow* (Does the service move in a clear direction?); *theme* (Does the service communicate a clear topic?); *transitions* (Does the service move well between different segments?); *variety* (Does the service include fresh forms?); and *concentration* (Does the length of the service fit the culture?).

Sixth, Christ-exalting worship is relevant to the culture. Jesus said worship was to be done "in spirit and truth" (John 4:24). This means worship must connect with worshipers' minds and wills. It must communicate the Word of God and connect with their emotions. It must meet both their intellects and their hearts. Among other things, worship must be culturally relevant. People desire to confess their sins, celebrate their faith, take communion, and sing in ways and manners that are their ways and manners. Christ-exalting worship draws people together so they are free to worship God in their own languages, cultural styles, and methods.

Seventh, Christ-exalting worship is concerned for the entire service, not just the sermon. The preaching of God's Word is of major importance. When it comes to corporate worship, the preaching of the Word of God must take priority over other aspects. Paul charged Timothy to "preach the word; be ready in season and out of season; reprove, rebuke, exhort, with great patience and instruction" (2 Tim. 4:2). Yet Paul also calls for balance in worship when he writes, "Let the word of Christ richly dwell within you [preaching], with all wisdom teaching and admonishing one another with psalms and hymns and spiritual songs [worship experience], singing with thankfulness in your hearts to God" (Col. 3:16). Churches design Christ-exalting worship services with the belief that the sermon is not the entire message, but the message is the entire service. Thus, the worship team works to develop a unified worship service that connects with people from the moment they walk into the auditorium until they exit it. This means the entire atmosphere is important to Christ-exalting worship (e.g., lighting, sound, smell, preaching, music, etc.). All these things matter in a worship service.

Eighth, Christ-exalting worship helps worshipers encounter God, see themselves in comparison to God, and respond to God's call on their lives (see Isa. 6:1–8). Throughout the Bible, people encountered or worshiped God in various ways and styles. Consider Moses at the burning bush, Abraham at the altar, Ezekiel at the river, or the apostle John on the isle of Patmos. Each worshiped God in a different manner. The common denominator? They were all changed! Well-known writer Gordon MacDonald suggests worship should be not about styles but outcomes. "The talk is all about style. What's missing is anyone asking, 'What effects does true worship have upon people?'"[6] The worship Isaiah experienced changed him. Worship expert William Epley notes the progression of Isaiah's worship experience through five phases. First, Isaiah saw God's majesty. Second, he confessed his need. Third, he received forgiveness. Fourth, he heard God's call to service. Fifth, he responded to God's call.[7] Isaiah left his worship experience a changed person ready to serve (continue to worship) God.

Five Types of Churches

Beginner Churches

Beginner churches take little effort in designing their worship services. The sermons, music, Scripture readings, and other elements are selected the week right before the worship service is offered. No thought is given to evaluating past services, and the music is simply considered preparation for the real activity—the sermon.

PLAN OF ACTION IF YOU LEAD A BEGINNER CHURCH

- Ask board members and worship leaders to answer the following question: What are the three most memorable experiences you have ever had in worship? Then discuss what made the experiences memorable and how the church might begin to include some of the insights in more of its services.
- Study the Bible to answer this question: What is worship?
- Recruit a worship team of at least three people: the lead pastor, worship leader, and a tech (sound, lights, communication) person.
- Plan all worship services two weeks in advance.

Novice Churches

Novice churches have started to ask the right questions about worship, including "What is biblical worship?" "What elements of worship should be included in a service?" "To whom is our worship service targeted?" The pastor plans sermons at least a month in advance to allow the worship leader more time to design a good worship experience. The pastor and worship leader meet at least once a quarter to evaluate and outline the next quarter of worship services.

Plan of Action If You Lead a Novice Church

- Ask board members and worship leaders to discuss and answer the following questions: Are there any ingredients in the act of true worship that ought to happen in every worship service? Which generation is the church seeking to reach? All generations? What does that mean for how the church designs worship? How much involvement and participation in worship should the church expect and invite?
- Plan all worship services one month in advance.

Intermediate Churches

Intermediate churches demonstrate a serious attitude toward their worship service design by planning three months in advance. The pastor of an intermediate church supports the early planning of worship by outlining the theme, Scripture, and essential direction of sermons three months in advance. A worship team of three to four people gathers monthly to evaluate past services and plan future services. Together the worship team determines to create genuine worship experiences for the congregation.

Plan of Action If You Lead an Intermediate Church

- Ask board members and worship leaders to discuss and answer the following questions: What is the difference between worship and praise? What are the legitimate needs of the people the church is trying to reach, and how can the church meet those needs through its worship service?
- Discuss what genuine worship should produce in worshipers.
- Plan all worship services three months in advance.
- Recruit and train at least two worship teams, allowing them to alternate in leading worship.

Advanced Churches

Advanced churches see worship as a performance where congregational members are the actors and God is the audience. Therefore, churches plan services to assist the congregation in respectfully honoring God while actively serving him through worship. Although worship teams keep a close eye on the response of newcomers, the members also focus on helping mature regular attendees in their faith. The pastor of an advanced church provides basic sermon outlines to the worship team six months in advance to enable long-range planning of services.

PLAN OF ACTION IF YOU LEAD AN ADVANCED CHURCH

- Ask board members and worship leaders to discuss and answer the following questions: Who is the audience for the worship service and who are the performers? How can the church keep maturing the people who attend worship?
- Outline all worship services six months in advance.
- Give careful thought to flow, pace, transitions, variety, and theme development in worship services.
- Recruit and train at least three worship teams, alternating them in leading worship.

Elite Churches

Elite churches seek the input of a large worship team with six or more members. The pastors of elite churches embrace worship planning by preparing basic sermon outlines a year in advance.

PLAN OF ACTION IF YOU LEAD AN ELITE CHURCH

- Ask board members and worship leaders to discuss and answer the following question: What outcomes are we seeing from our worship services?

- Outline all worship services a year in advance.
- Organize worship around a clear, dominant theme with good pace, flow, and transitions.
- Find ways to involve people in actively worshiping God rather than just being spectators at a concert.
- Recruit and train multiple worship teams to lead worship in the services.

Eddie Gibbs, former professor of Church Growth, declares that inspiring worship exists when "church members are eager to come. They are reluctant to be absent from a service in case they miss anything. As a result of their coming to the service, they go home refreshed and better able to face the week."[8] Fit churches reach people with culturally relevant music and worship.

Main Points

- *Beginner church*: gives little thought and time to planning the worship experience.
- *Novice church*: recognizes the importance of intentional worship planning and takes steps to move toward a more intentional approach.
- *Intermediate church*: pastors initiate better planning and evaluation of the worship experience.
- *Advanced church*: views worship as essential in assisting the congregation in connecting with God.
- *Elite church*: expends great time and effort to make sure it does everything humanly possible to ensure a connectional worship experience, while reliance on the Holy Spirit is evident.

DISCIPLE-MAKING
STRATEGIES

Muscular endurance involves muscle groups repeatedly exert-
ing force against resistance. Fit churches need to develop their
ability to exert force against resistance. Many aspects of life can
cause resistance in the life of Christ followers. In an attempt
to stay in step with the Spirit (see Gal. 5:25), both inside and
outside forces exert resistance on the believer's ability to follow Christ.

Satan applies resistance. "Stay alert! Watch out for your great
enemy, the devil. He prowls around like a roaring lion, looking
for someone to devour" (1 Pet. 5:8 NLT). The world in which
you are called to live pushes back on you. "Don't copy the behavior and customs of this world" (Rom. 12:2 NLT). You get
resistance from your own desires that if not checked will result
in sin. "Temptation comes from our own desires, which entice
us and drag us away. These desires give birth to sinful actions.
And when sin is allowed to grow, it gives birth to death" (James

> **You might be a fit church if . . .**
>
> - You read through the Gospels and clearly defined a disciple.
> - You have developed a strategy for making disciples.
> - You have started at least five disciple-making groups.
> - You have embraced a process of making disciples throughout the entire congregation.
> - You expect all leaders to have an apprentice whom they are discipling.
> - You value disciple-making with time and budget.
> - You are seeing disciples multiplied.

1:14–15 NLT). You must develop spiritual muscle to exert force against such resistance.

Disciple-making is a central component for developing muscular endurance. Christ's commission to his church underscored this. "Go therefore and make disciples" (Matt. 28:19) is the clear clarion call of Christ. Few churches deny this, but few churches design strategies to make it happen.

Paul instructed Timothy, "My dear son, be strong through the grace that God gives you in Christ Jesus. You have heard me teach things that have been confirmed by many reliable witnesses. Now teach these truths to other trustworthy people who will be able to pass them on to others" (2 Tim. 2:1–2 NLT). Paul was providing Timothy with a basic strategic framework for disciple-making. The basics being this: take what you have learned and share with those who will pass it to others.

A church that is effectively building the body will design and deploy disciple-making strategies. "We can measure a church's spiritual health and its ultimate success by its obedience to the Great Commission."[1] A healthy, fit church is one that is making disciples. And it uses a disciple-making process, not a disciple-making program, to create multiplying disciples!

The Genesis of Disciple-Making

The genesis of disciple-making is the leader. You cannot make disciples until you are a disciple. You cannot challenge others to be followers of Christ unless you are a follower of Christ. It is out of your *followership* that you lead others to follow. "The truth is that the greatest way to create a movement is to be a follower and to show others how to follow. Following is the most underrated form of leadership in existence."[2] Paul said to those he led, "Follow my example, as I follow the example of Christ" (1 Cor. 11:1 NIV). Craig Groeschel, the lead pastor of Life Church in Oklahoma City, explains, "We have too many full-time pastors who are part-time followers of Christ. What we need are more part-time pastors who are full-time followers of Christ."[3] He was not making a case for bivocational ministry but instead was making the point that pastors are to be followers of Jesus first. Then they are to pastor/lead their churches.

Church leaders, you are the genesis, epicenter, core of the disciple-making aspect of your church. You must be in a discipling relationship and you must be discipling others. From your modeling of discipleship and living as a disciple, your church will progress toward fitness in this area. Out of your connection with God you are able to influence others to connect with him too. "The only enduring influence we have to offer others is the influence God has in our lives."[4] What are you doing to increase being influenced by God?

In his book *Strategic Disciple Making*, Aubrey Malphurs identifies four competencies a leader can, and must, bring to the disciple-making process: character (being), knowledge (knowing), skills (doing), and emotions (feeling). "Achieving excellence in all four competencies must take place for the leaders to be able to do their jobs effectively,"[5] he writes. Honing each of these allows the leader to influence at a higher level.

In Phil's role as a district superintendent, he made an interesting discovery: many of the pastors under his oversight had never been discipled. As a result, many of his churches had anemic, if any, disciple-making strategies. People were going through the motions of programmatic disciple-making but were seeing little authentic transformation.

He determined to address this issue and developed Disciple-Making Leadership Communities (DMLC). This was one-year, intensive peer disciple-making for pastors. The purpose was to teach pastors the skills and show them the heart it takes to be followers of Christ. The idea was that if pastors could become more passionate about following Jesus, develop skills for listening to the voice of God, and experience daily spiritual transformation, then a movement of reproducible disciple-making might result.

At the writing of this book, Phil was just beginning the second generation of the DMLC. Honestly, he still has difficulty convincing his pastors of the value of disciple-making. Many pastors still view it as merely finding the right material to teach. And, frankly, some who have completed the year-long intensive have yet to reproduce it in their churches. But those who have reproduced it have seen transformational things happen in their lives and in the lives of those in their church. The results have proven one thing without a doubt: if discipleship is to happen in a church, it must begin with the pastor.

Define a Disciple

During a diving competition at the 2016 Rio Olympics, one of the television commentators made an interesting comment. He said that in training divers, the first thing the Chinese do is teach their divers how to enter the water from whatever diving apparatus they are competing from (e.g., springboard, platform, etc.). Prior to any work on flips, turns, somersaults, and other aspects of technique, divers are coached on how to enter the water. The result is that Chinese divers enter the water with minimal splash, and minimal splash is a critical element of scoring high marks.

In essence, the Chinese divers start with the end in mind. Everything else is built on the conclusion of the dive. If they know how to end well, everything leading up to the ending creates a solid performance.

You need to apply this same principle to the disciple-making process. You need to know what you are looking for in a disciple. What does a disciple look like? What actions, attitudes, and attributes do you want in a follower of Jesus? "You need to define what you want to accomplish and how you are going to do it."[6] Clarity as to the end result will inform the process you put in place to get there.

According to Aubrey Malphurs, "In a specific sense, a disciple is one who has trusted in Christ as Savior."[7] This provides a foundation for what it means to be a disciple, but it does not clarify what that person who trusts Jesus might look like. To gain a better handle on disciple-making, more specifics must be provided.

In the book *DiscipleShift*, authors Jim Putnam and Bobby Harrington provide two practical guidelines for defining a disciple. "First, the definition needs to be *biblical* (as Jesus defined it), and second, it needs to be *clear*."[8] Using Matthew 4:19 as a pivot point, they provide three key characteristics of a disciple. Jesus stated, "Come, follow me, and I will send you out to fish for people" (Matt. 4:19 NIV).

The three characteristics, or attributes, of a disciple are: a disciple follows Jesus, a disciple is changed by Jesus, and a disciple is on a mission with Jesus. Putnam and Harrington define a disciple as an individual who is "following Christ, being changed by Christ, and is committed to the mission of Christ."[9] The drive to produce these attributes informs Putnam and Harrington's disciple-making process.

Regardless of the definition you give to a disciple, the most basic characteristic of a disciple is obedience. This characteristic is seen in John 2. It is in the story of Jesus turning water into wine that obedience is specified. Mary, the mother of Jesus, told the servants, "Do whatever he tells you" (v. 5 NLT). Obedience without hesitation to Jesus's instructions is the primary mark of a disciple. "Basic to all discipleship is our resolve not only to address Jesus with polite titles but to follow his teaching and obey his commands."[10] In all the effort put into a definition of a disciple, obedience is an observable action.

When working on producing disciples you will want to answer these three questions: "What qualities and behaviors are we trying to develop in disciples? What do we want them to do? What do we want them to be?"[11] What is clear is that a church building the body defines an end result to the disciple-making process.

Elements of a Disciple-Making Strategy

Jesus's clear and compelling invitation to "come, follow me" has not changed. These three words opened the door to transformational living for those to whom he extended it. These three words demanded a response. These three words set people into motion on the path of discipleship.

The invite was distinct. The invite was full of challenge. The invite was consistent, no matter the person or situation. The impact of the invite was dependent on the response of the one who was extended the invitation.

When Jesus crossed paths with Peter and Andrew, he shared the invitation to follow him. Upon hearing Jesus's words, "They left their nets at once and followed him" (Matt. 4:20 NLT). Jesus's invitation resulted in them letting go of "what was" to discover "what could be."

In another conversation, Jesus extended an invitation for a rich man to follow him (see Mark 10:17–31). The rich man's first response was enthusiastic, but Jesus noted something in him and added a challenge to his invitation. The challenge was for the man to first sell all he had, then follow him. This dampened the man's enthusiasm. "At this the man's face fell, and he went away sad, for he had many possessions" (v. 22 NLT). This rich man responded to Jesus's invite by holding on to what was at the expense of what could be. His willingness to follow Jesus was contingent on minimal risk.

Jesus's invitation to follow him has not changed. Those who respond, as Peter and Andrew did, set out on the path of discipleship. Now the question becomes, How do we effectively make disciples at this time in God's history?

The following five key principles influence and determine the process, structure, and material for effective disciple-making:

Effective disciple-making is relational. People are discipled in relationship, not in the transference of knowledge or content.

Effective disciple-making is biblical. The Word of God is central to making disciples. A disciple is a follower of Christ. How better to understand who you follow than to read about who he was, how he thought, and what he did.

Effective disciple-making is applicable. If a disciple-making process does not impact how people live in the world, then it is merely religious ritual. Disciples bring the kingdom of God into the areas of life where they have been placed.

Effective disciple-making is accountable. Accountability is often an underutilized component of the disciple-making process. Accountability goes beyond getting assignments completed; it means holding those serious about following Christ accountable to live out their following him in daily life.

Effective disciple-making is reproducible. Reproducing other disciples is often the missing piece of disciple-making. Genuine disciple-making has happened when other disciples have been multiplied. The growing and making of disciples is a lifelong process.

These five principles are the filter used in developing, implementing, and evaluating disciple-making in your ministry. So regularly ask the following five questions regarding disciple-making in your church:

- What is the relational impact?
- How is the Bible used?
- How is the disciple-making process impacting how people live in the world?
- How are people being held accountable?
- How is what we're doing reproducing disciples?

Disciple-making is the call of every Christ follower. The call to "go and make disciples" continues to be the intent of Jesus's mandate to his church (Matt. 28:19 NLT). What will you do to fulfill this mandate in your life and in the lives of those in the faith communities you lead?

Five Types of Churches

Beginner Churches

Beginner churches affirm disciple-making but seldom have well-thought-out processes in place. These churches see the pastor's teaching as the primary discipling methodology. If anything is in place outside the pulpit teaching, it primarily involves the pastor meeting with folks one-on-one or in groups. The leadership of beginner churches is always on the lookout for the best packaged material they might use.

PLAN OF ACTION IF YOU LEAD A BEGINNER CHURCH

- Identify the church's current disciple-making process.
- The pastor gets involved in a group where people can be discipled.
- The pastor and board read through the Gospels looking for how Jesus defined a disciple.
- Make a list of three to five admirable characteristics to be produced in the life of a disciple.
- The pastor and board read one book on disciple-making.

Novice Churches

Novice churches are aware of the inadequacy of a pulpit-driven disciple-making process. The leaders have started to develop observable criteria for what makes a disciple. The pastoral teams have been exposed to books on disciple-making and are getting greater clarity on the principles of disciple-making. Novice churches are beginning to put plans in place.

PLAN OF ACTION IF YOU LEAD A NOVICE CHURCH

- Key leaders should study a book on disciple-making.
- The leadership of the church (pastor, pastoral staff, and board) define and agree on the definition of a disciple for the church.
- Develop a first draft of a disciple-making process to achieve the agreed on end result.
- Key leaders should participate in the draft process.
- Evaluate the effectiveness of the process.
- Retool the process as necessary.

Intermediate Churches

Intermediate churches have achieved agreement across their leadership teams on the definition of a disciple. The leadership has test-run the church's disciple-making process, evaluated it, and retooled it. A second cohort of leaders is now experiencing the revised discipleship process, and the wider church body is sensing the importance and necessity of a genuine disciple-making strategy.

PLAN OF ACTION IF YOU LEAD AN INTERMEDIATE CHURCH

- Pastor should preach a sermon series on what it means to be a disciple.
- The leaders who have been through the initial disciple-making process need to lead a group of three to five people through the revised process.
- The head pastor leads another disciple-making group.
- Make the expectation of being discipled an element of the church's DNA.

Advanced Churches

Advanced churches are populated with disciple-making groups. These groups are designed around both knowing about and practicing discipleship. These churches have a built-in expectation that people who have been discipled will disciple others. Disciple-making is woven into every aspect of the church.

PLAN OF ACTION IF YOU LEAD AN ADVANCED CHURCH

- Pastor should teach a regular pulpit series on biblical disciple-making.
- Evaluate how many of those who have been discipled have discipled others.
- Evaluate the church's disciple-making process.
- Build disciple-making into the church's membership expectations.

Elite Churches

Elite churches are multiplying disciple-making into the third and fourth generations. These churches define effectiveness according to how many are multiplying disciples, not merely how many are being discipled. The pastoral leadership teams are consistently discipling others. Many of those who have been discipled are going out to begin new faith communities. Elite churches have an intentional process that multiplies disciples, leaders, and churches.

PLAN OF ACTION IF YOU LEAD AN ELITE CHURCH

- Revisit your church's definition of a disciple. What may need to be changed or clarified?
- Evaluate how your church's process is working in regard to developing the disciples it wants.
- Share with other churches what your church has learned regarding disciple-making.
- Determine ways you might engage more in the disciple-making process.

Disciple-making contributes greatly to a church moving toward fitness and health. "The solution to our ineffectiveness as churches involves following a clear and uncomplicated way to train people to be spiritually mature, fully devoted followers of Christ, then in turn having those disciples make more disciples."[12] Churches that are building the body take seriously the call to make disciples who make disciples, who make disciples.

Main Points

- *Beginner church*: affirms disciple-making.
- *Novice church*: explores how disciple-making can be implemented.
- *Intermediate church*: disciples leaders.
- *Advanced church*: multiplies disciples.
- *Elite church*: multiplies churches through the disciple-making process.

Pastoral Leadership

Phil served on staff with John Maxwell from 1982 to 1988. John would often tell the staff that "everything rises and falls on leadership." A church that has made the decision to increase its fitness level needs someone to point the way forward. The pastor is an elder and has an obligation and opportunity to lead their church under Christ's authority. While Jesus is the ultimate leader of every congregation (see 1 Pet. 5:4), each congregation has human leaders (elders) who are to "shepherd the flock of God among you, exercising oversight" (v. 2). The need for human leaders cannot be shunned or ignored. A leaderless church drifts much like the person of divided loyalty described in James 1:6: "Do not waver, for a person with divided loyalty is as unsettled as a wave of the sea that is blown and tossed by the wind" (NLT). A church with leadership that is blown and tossed by the waves of uncertainty will never make headway or progress. The pastor must make the decision to step up and lead the congregation.

Pastors have many responsibilities and often neglect the responsibility to lead. "Pastors, by and large, do an excellent job

You might be a fit church if . . .

- Your sermons help the church fulfill its mission and vision.
- You lead with a clear, personal call from God.
- You pursue personal and professional growth and development.
- You communicate a well-defined vision that captures people's imaginations.
- You manage conflict well to preserve the unity of the church.
- You embrace and lead appropriate change based on the church's vision.
- You are a team player who actively involves others in ministry.

of everything but their most important duty—leading."[1] Pastors often fail to fulfill the important role of leading for two reasons: they accept the number one leadership myth as truth and they avoid embracing the responsibility for achieving results.

Number-One Leadership Myth

The number-one leadership myth is that leaders are born, not made. A pastor may neglect his responsibility to lead the church because he feels he is not a born leader.

In fact, often the first question I hear pastors ask at leadership conferences is this: Do you believe leaders can be developed? They are basically asking this: Are leaders made or born? It is accurate to say that some people are born with a propensity toward leadership because of some natural giftedness and personality. But anyone who chooses to learn can increase their leadership capacity. Indeed, anyone can ramp up their leadership ability.

In their book *The Truth about Leadership*, educators James Kouzes and Barry Posner report, "After examining the immense variety of stories from so many different people and places, it has also become crystal clear that *leadership is not a birthright* (emphasis added)."[2] This underscores the demythization that leaders are born, not made. The sooner pastors recognize they can develop leadership capacity and competency, the more willing they will be to develop the skills necessary to lead a church to fitness.

Avoiding the Responsibility

The second most common reason a pastor may neglect to lead his church is a tendency to avoid accepting responsibility for achieving results. Often a pastor couches his reasoning in spiritual terms. He believes God brings the harvest, God is the one who saves, and Jesus will build his church, not us. This is all true, but it is also true that God works in partnership with human leaders. For example, in the parable of the sower, what begins the process of reaping a harvest? It is the action of the farmer! "Listen! A *farmer went out* to plant some seeds . . . *he scattered* them across his field" (Matt. 13:3–4 NLT, emphasis added). The farmer (leader) *went out* and *scattered*. All the seeds did not sprout, but some germinated and grew. And while God produced the fruit, you can be 100 percent certain that if the farmer had done nothing, nothing would have resulted.

Paul makes this same point to the church in Corinth. "After all, who is Apollos? Who is Paul? We are only God's servants through whom you believed the Good News. Each of us did the work the Lord gave us. I planted the seed in your hearts, and Apollos watered it, but it was God who made it grow" (1 Cor. 3:5–6 NLT). God did indeed make the seed grow, but someone (a leader) needed to plant or water it—sometimes both. And God provided the growth.

A pastor cannot and must not avoid responsibility in the work God desires to do in the life of the church he has given the pastor to lead. When God was responding to the cries of his people in captivity, he called Moses (a leader) to partner with him. God said to Moses, "Then the LORD told him, 'I have certainly seen the oppression of my people in Egypt. I have heard their cries of distress because of their harsh slave drivers. Yes, I am aware of their suffering. So I have come down to rescue them from the power of the Egyptians and lead them out of Egypt into their own fertile and spacious land'" (Exod. 3:7–8 NLT). God saw the need and took action.

His action was not unilateral. It was not exercised in a *divine vacuum*. He said to Moses, "Now go, for I am sending you to Pharaoh. You must lead my people Israel out of Egypt" (v. 10 NLT). God was going to do it, but he was going to do it through Moses. What God desires to do through your church, he desires to do through you. The call he has on your church to bring it to greater fitness is for you to lead. The call he has on your church to make it more effective for the Great Commission is for you to lead.

Pastoral leadership is an aspect of muscular endurance. Physically, muscular endurance is the ability of a muscle or a group of muscles to repeatedly exert force against resistance. You will experience resistance as you move the church toward an increased level of fitness. You will find resistance as the necessary fitness plans are put into place. The exertion of your pastoral leadership in dealing with the resistance will be the difference between increasing fitness and remaining static.

Take Responsibility to Lead

In running, distance is constant, i.e., a mile is a mile. The variable is the time in which the mile is navigated. The time is impacted by the runner's level of fitness, the terrain that makes up the mile, and the weather (e.g., temperature, wind, snow, or rain). Each variable impacts the time in which the mile is run. It is true that running on a treadmill can negate some of the variables, but leading a church is seldom like running on a treadmill. Few things in a church can be set to remain consistent.

The need for leadership in each of the five types of churches, however, is a constant. Pastors need to lead. The variable is the context in which they lead. "We tell our audiences that as much as the context of leadership has changed, the content of leadership has not changed that much at all."[3] This being the case, how you lead in each of the five types will vary. A leader needs to decide the type of church they have and the church's level of fitness and then devise a plan to move to the next level.

Pastoral leadership is critical in providing muscular endurance. When a church goes through the five stages, it will confront resistance. It is through intentional leadership that the resistance, when encountered, will be overcome. This resistance aids in the strengthening of the local church. Much like a muscle gains strength and tone when it repeatedly exerts force against resistance, a church is strengthened and toned by pushing through the resistance it faces.

When you lead your church toward an elite status, you will experience many challenges and difficulties. In the initial stages, minimal resistance may feel like too much to handle, but if you continue the effort, soon you will move to a heightened level of corporate strength and tone.

Baseline Fitness Factors

Most exercise programs recommend that a person consult a doctor prior to beginning strenuous activity. The purpose behind this is so the person can properly determine what level of activity they can engage in. When you go to see a doctor, they check three baselines of health. Regardless of your reason for the visit, the same three baselines are monitored: temperature, blood pressure, and weight.

Why these three? Each is an indicator of what the body is doing. These three do not tell the whole story, but they do provide indicators of trends. Establishing a baseline is critical in all health evaluations.

Do churches have baselines? The short answer is yes! The three baselines of church fitness are: salvations, baptisms, and funds invested in disciple-making initiatives. These three do not tell the entire story, but they do provide a snapshot as to the relative fitness level of a church. A leader should measure these three baselines as a guide to where his church is and how he might need to lead.

The guidelines for measuring the baseline factors are as follows. Salvations are a percentage of weekend worship participation. Baptisms are a percentage of those reported as being saved. The disciple-making investment is the percentage of a church's annual budget invested in disciple-making processes and strategies. This investment includes evangelism and discipleship materials, promotional material, and training tools. The specifics of each baseline factor are delineated as each of the five types of churches is unpacked.

Five Types of Churches

Beginner Churches

Beginner churches are very sedentary and have low fitness levels. They have been involved in minimal missional activity. Like beginning runners, beginner churches are not prepared to walk a mile, much less run a marathon.

The baseline fitness factors for beginner churches might look like the following. They will have zero salvations and zero baptisms in a twelve-month period. If any funds are budgeted for disciple-making, normally less than one percent is designated.

This is equivalent to individuals whose physical activity has involved the least amount of exertion possible. In beginner churches, muscular endurance is extremely underdeveloped. The slightest exertion will result in resistance and soreness. Few churches, like people, enjoy the aches and pains associated with becoming healthier and fit. Most churches simply like the idea of being more effective but prefer not to do the work required.

The primary role of pastoral leadership in a beginner church is to determine how dissatisfied the church is with its current fitness level. A one-word definition of motivation is dissatisfaction. Until a church is dissatisfied with where it is, it will not be motivated to do anything.

Jesus modeled this when he encountered the man by the pool of Bethesda. The man was there because people believed the pool provided healing powers; when the waters stirred, the first one in would be healed. As you might imagine, it became a popular place. In John 5, we read, "One of the men lying there had been sick for thirty-eight years. When Jesus saw him and knew he had been ill for a long time, he asked him, 'Would you like to get well?'" (John 5:5–6 NLT). Jesus knew the man had been ill for a long time, but he still asked him if he was interested in getting well. Jesus wanted to determine his level of dissatisfaction. Why? Not everyone who is sick wants to get better. Similarly, not every church that is unhealthy or in need of more physical activity is motivated to change.

Remember how Phil needed to come to a point of dissatisfaction before his motivation kicked in to start living a fit lifestyle? His moment of dissatisfaction came when he realized he would avoid, as much as possible, looking at himself in a mirror. He had gotten so heavy and out of shape that seeing himself was too convicting. Phil's initial response was simply to avoid anything that might reflect his reality. Fortunately, he decided to change the reflection instead of avoiding it forever.

You need to find the mirror, or picture, that will stir the waters of dissatisfaction in your congregation. Beginner churches must see it is necessary to change and move toward higher levels of fitness. They must be motivated. Part of your job is to help your church see reality! When you help your church recognize its dissatisfaction, you will create motivation.

Plan of Action If You Lead a Beginner Church

- Teach on Great Commission initiatives.
- Evaluate the past twelve months and clearly determine the number of salvations and baptisms.
- Evaluate the budget and determine what percentage the church is using for disciple-making initiatives.

Novice Churches

Novice churches have begun to get more active. They have moved from a primarily sedentary role to one of moderate activity. Like novice runners who are capable of running one to three miles at a pace that is good for them, novice churches are following a plan and exercising three to five days per week.

These churches are engaging in regular evangelistic endeavors and have a heart for the communities in which they serve. Missional activity is also gaining traction. They are implementing ministry at a pace they can handle and have begun to have a higher sense of corporate self-esteem.

The baseline fitness factors for novice churches are salvations of 1–3 percent of weekend worship participation, baptisms of 10–15 percent of salvations reported, and budgeted 3–5 percent of the yearly income toward disciple-making initiatives.

Pastoral leadership roles in novice churches must develop a plan that will move the church toward a lifestyle of fitness. Leaders must take what the church understands about church health and growth and put the knowledge into practice. A key component is training.

Training in novice churches should include personal sharing of one's faith story, leadership, discipleship, foundations in Christian living, and the power of involvement in faith communities. It is incumbent on each church's pastoral leader to know where he can push the church. Work done at this stage lays a foundation for the church to move into the intermediate stage of church growth and vitality.

Plan of Action If You Lead a Novice Church

- Determine the training that is most needed.
- Develop a training program on this element.
- Have the leadership team go through this training.
- Get feedback.
- Provide the training for a larger segment of the church.

Intermediate Churches

Intermediate churches are able to consistently and constantly engage in missional, externally focused activities. They have built up the spiritual stamina to sustain a higher pace than novice churches, similar to how intermediate runners are capable of running thirty minutes at a nine-minute-per-mile pace. Intermediate churches are both consistent (time) and constant (duration).

The pastoral leadership role in intermediate churches is to show progress. Dissatisfaction is definitely the key motivator in the beginning, but achievement is the long-term motivator. You have to show other church leaders they are making progress. Progress is the fuel of steadfastness. Progress is the mile markers on the road to a church's destination. When a church knows it is making progress, it is motivated to continue.

Plan of Action If You Lead an Intermediate Church

- Decide how the church will define progress.
- Design the system to measure progress.
- Develop a means to report the progress being made.
- Encourage church leaders to keep moving forward.

Advanced Churches

Advanced churches are at a high level of fitness. Like advanced runners, churches at this point are both students and teachers. Advanced runners consistently push themselves toward new heights of running fitness. They look for challenges. They are constantly learning, and they choose not only to develop themselves but also to help others.

Thus, advanced churches help start other churches. They are radical, outward-looking churches. They are fit and healthy enough to raise up and send out people. They are similar to the church in Antioch that raised up Paul and Barnabas and sent them out. "So after more fasting and prayer, the men laid their hands on them [Paul and Barnabas] and sent them on their way" (Acts 13:3 NLT). Advanced churches are sending churches.

Church planters Todd Wilson and Dave Ferguson feel advanced churches "demonstrate the ability to reproduce leaders, services, and sites/campuses."[4] Advanced churches are fit enough, healthy enough, and confident enough to multiply disciples, leaders, and churches.

The role of pastoral leaders in advanced churches is to challenge the church with expanded vision. You must help the church see God's kingdom is about expansion, and you must not confuse a vision with a dream.

The vision is what the dream looks like when it is achieved. It is definable, measurable, and achievable. A dream is drawing attention to the horizon. A vision is drawing attention to a particular point on the horizon. In advanced churches, you must have a point on the horizon. If you do not, the church will wander and begin to lose its fitness.

Plan of Action If You Lead an Advanced Church

- Clarify the need for a vision.
- Embrace the church's vision.
- Refine the vision.
- Share the vision.
- Have others offer ideas about the vision.

Elite Churches

Elite churches have few models to follow. Therefore, they look not for models but for peers—peers that have achieved the same level of effectiveness. Then peer-learning communities are established. In these communities, shared learning is embraced, but the learning is meant not just for the elite churches—it is so they can invest in others. Just as there are few elite runners, there are few elite churches. In the 2016 Olympics, "There [were] 554 Americans competing in Rio, comprising 0.00017 percent of the US population."[5] This fact points to the rarity of elite athletes. Likewise, elite churches make up a very small percentage of all churches, perhaps 1–2 percent of all churches, at most.

The pastoral leadership role in elite churches is that of spiritual executive officer (SEO). There was a time when the position of chief executive officer (CEO) was thought to be the model for leaders in elite churches, but it is not enough to be the CEO in these churches. You have to be the SEO.

You have to stay connected to God so you can keep your church connected to him. You have to be a Christ follower so you can engender others to be followers of Christ. You have to open yourself up to the Spirit of God so you can get in tune with him.

Paul challenges leaders in this way: "Since we are living by the Spirit, let us follow the Spirit's leading in every part of our lives" (Gal. 5:25 NLT). This is what a SEO does—follows the leading of the Spirit.

When you lead as a SEO, you must be *open* to hear what God is saying, *ready* to discern what you are hearing, and *brave* to act on what you discern.

PLAN OF ACTION IF YOU LEAD AN ELITE CHURCH

The pastor as SEO of the church should do the following:

- Know how people consistently connect with God.
- Spend regular time in listening to the Spirit.
- Record what they are hearing.
- Lead from a listening posture.

Pastoral leadership is an essential ingredient in building the body. At each level of church is a primary role of pastoral leadership.

Main Points

- *Beginner church*: the pastor helps the church recognize areas of dissatisfaction.
- *Novice church*: the pastor works with leaders in the church to develop a plan to move toward fitness.
- *Intermediate church*: identifies clear markers that show progress toward fitness.
- *Advanced church*: expands visionary capacity to starting new churches.
- *Elite church*: the pastor leads as a spiritual executive officer (SEO).

PART 4

Flexibility

The more flexible a muscle group, the less likelihood of injury. Likewise, the more flexible a church is, the more likely it is to adapt to disciple-making opportunities. Churches need to be flexible to adapt and stretch and embrace new challenges. The characteristics that contribute to the flexibility of a church body are loving community, vision-directed systems, and divine empowerment. When the Spirit guides a church, when a faith community develops its systems and processes around vision, it becomes agile and flexible, making it able to avoid injury brought on by shortsightedness and stubbornness.

10

LOVING COMMUNITY

Gary's friend was visiting a church recently and casually took a seat about midway toward the front of the worship center. Like most people, he prefers a seat on the aisle and took the first seat in the row of chairs. Within a few minutes, he noticed a woman walk past him and glance at the exact seat where he was sitting. She walked to the front of the auditorium and back again twice, each time glancing in his direction. On her third trip down the aisle, she stopped and asked, "Young man, are you going to be sitting there?" The friend replied that, yes, he was planning to sit there throughout the worship service. She then asked, "Would you mind moving? You see, that is my normal seat, and I'd like to sit there." Even though he thought this was odd behavior, Gary's friend decided it would be best if he moved. Since numerous other seats were available, he simply sat down in the row immediately in front of where he had been sitting.

No doubt, we all have experienced a similar situation in our own churches. We are creatures of habit, and we like to sit in the same familiar place week after week. In larger churches, it may not be as apparent, but particularly in smaller churches the

---

You might be a fit church if . . .

- You nurture an atmosphere of acceptance and love among the people.
- You have an effective connecting ministry.
- You offer a small group ministry that involves over 66 percent of your people.
- You welcome and follow up with guests well.
- You help people make friends in the congregation.
- You handle conflict well.
- You provide regular opportunities for fellowship and community.

---

pastor can tell who is absent just by observing who is not sitting in their normal places.

"May I have your seat?" People answer yes to this question in churches with loving communities of faith.

Room for Me?

Have you ever wondered why people attend and remain at your church? In most communities in North America, people could support any number of churches. People do not have to attend church. Rather, it is a matter of choice. One factor that influences people to remain at a church is the sense of it being a loving community, and several questions come into play when people evaluate whether a church is a loving community.

Does the Church Have Room for Me Physically?

A few weeks ago when Gary was consulting with a church, during the worship service he quietly slipped out and walked through the parking lot. While he was observing the parking situation, two people drove into the lot and circled around looking for a parking space. When they could not find one, they returned to the exit and left. If guests do not perceive a church has enough room for them, they leave or do not return for a second visit. People notice if a church meets their needs regarding ease of traversing the buildings and campus. If a building has too many stairs, ice is not removed from walkways in the winter, or restrooms are not handicap accessible, people may not want to attend that church.

Does the Church Have Room for Me Culturally?

Today there is a great need for churches that are culturally appropriate, but what is considered culturally appropriate covers a wide span of thinking. Consider two key aspects of cultural fit. First, when guests attend your church, one thing they do is look around to see if others in attendance look like them. Newcomers want to know if others have similar backgrounds or are in similar life stages. They hope to find people who have the same interests. And they particularly look for specialty groups that meet their needs. Second, when guests attend your church, they expect it to be contemporary in the best sense of that term. Cultural observer and anthropologist Charles Kraft defines a contemporary church as one that impresses "the uninitiated observer as an original production of the contemporary culture, not as a badly fitted import from somewhere else."[1] Otherwise, people want the atmosphere to have the look and feel of home. Is the church somewhere people feel *in place* or *out of place*? To use a missionary term, is the church indigenous?

Does the Church Have Room for Me Relationally?

Fit churches are characterized by joy, warmth, love, and expressions of genuine happiness. Yet people desire more than a friendly church. What they really want are friends. Many individuals grew up in a milieu of broken relationships, divorce, and loneliness. They are looking for family, and the church is the perfect place for them to receive this type of connection. They are highly committed to their friends and relationships. For many, friends are the only stable family they know. After attending your church for a few weeks, people notice if members are making room for them in the various classes and/or small groups. They will discover whether the cliques can be penetrated or if groups and classes are closed off to them. People want to connect with the teachers, the small group leaders, and the people—not just the content.

Does the Church Have Room for Me Actively?

Too often in modern churches the professionals do ministry and the people sit and watch or take notes. This type of passive classroom approach to church is not appropriate today. People do not simply want to study spirituality; they want to be immersed in it. In other words, they want the lab first and then the lecture. In addition, they want to participate fully in their own spirituality. They do not want a professional to talk to God and then tell them about it. People wish to immerse themselves in the event, experience, and topic they are studying. This is really no different from elements of our normal experience. When Gary wanted to play basketball for his high school team, he did not aspire to sit in a class listening to a coach lecture about basketball; he wanted to play the game and be coached on how to play better.

Is Church Worth My Time?

The demand on people's time in our society is strong. Once people begin attending your church, they will ask, "Is it worth my time to attend?" and "Is it worth my time to participate in the ministry?" People will judge whether to become involved in worship, ministry, classes, or groups based on how each meets their specific needs.

Needs of People

An old Jewish story tells of a rabbi who asked the Lord to show him heaven and hell. "I will show you hell," said the Lord as he opened the door to a room. Inside was a large round table with a pot of delicious stew in the center. The people in the room were equipped with long-handled spoons, but they were starving. They were able to dip the spoons into the stew quite easily, but because the spoon handles were longer than a person's arm, they were unable to get the nourishing food to their mouths.

"Now I will show you heaven," said the Lord. This time the rabbi saw a room identical to the first, except the people were well-nourished, laughing, and talking. They had the same long-handled spoons but somehow had overcome this handicap. To the puzzled rabbi, the Lord explained, "It's simple but requires a certain skill—they have learned to feed each other." The people in heaven were obviously prospering in an atmosphere of giving and receiving. If someone would refuse to give and receive, the system would collapse.

The story illustrates a central need for members of any church—everyone needs to be willing to give and to receive. However, you should address the following needs if your church is to be fit.

A Sense of Belonging

The world we live in is marked by loneliness. To combat the loss of community, some people go to nightclubs, others become overly involved in volunteer organizations, still others go anywhere they can to be around people. For example, they make a daily visit to the bank or the mall. God expects Christians to band together, caring, loving, and growing into a community where relationships are not superficial but penetrating and meaningful.

A Sense of Purpose

When members understand the biblical reasons for a church and their participation in it, they develop a sense of purpose. Personal growth is most effectively accomplished through a group of Christians who are committed to Christ, one another, and ministry in the world.

A Knowledge of What Is Expected

All churches have rules, often called norms, under which members agree to abide while in the church. Members must have a part in determining these rules so they can live and work effectively toward the group goals. In some clear detail, church members must know what the church expects of them so they can participate in a confident manner.

A Part in Planning the Future

People need to play a part in structuring the church's overall plans and goals. This need is satisfied when their ideas get a fair hearing. Goals and plans must be within reach; if members sense the plans cannot be reasonably accomplished, then they will lose heart in the church.

A Challenging Atmosphere

Because of time constraints, people must make choices regarding how they use their time. For people to remain involved in a church, they must feel challenged in their thinking and in how they use their gifts. They must feel stretched within the range of their abilities and interests, and they must trust their work in the church will lead to the accomplishment of its goals.

An Understanding of What Is Going On

Members need to be kept informed. What people are not informed about, they often oppose. Keeping members informed is one way to give them status as individuals. Leaders usually think they have communicated effectively, but those who listen sometimes find they do not understand what is being stated. The following humorous story will serve as an illustration.

At the height of the vacation season one year, a trained investigator mingled with the crowds at Grand Central Station in New

York City. He asked, "What is your destination?" of ten people and received the following responses: "Protestant." "Mind your own business." "I'm a shoe salesman." "Home, if I can find my wife." "I'm learning to be a mail clerk." "Checkers." "Shut your mouth." "I don't know you." "Hoboken." And "I believe in faith, hope, and charity."

Obviously, we must never assume we have communicated to the members of our church.

In the fall, when you see geese flying south for the winter, they will most likely be in a "V" formation. They fly that way naturally. As each bird flaps its wings, it creates an uplift for the bird immediately behind. By using this flying formation, the entire flock adds about 71 percent greater flying range than if each bird flew alone.

When a goose falls out of formation, it suddenly feels the draft of trying to go it alone and quickly returns to the formation to take advantage of the lifting power of the flock. As the lead goose gets tired, he rotates back in the formation and another goose flies the point.

If a goose becomes sick or wounded and falls out of formation, two geese fall out and follow him down to provide assistance and protection. They stay with the fallen goose until it is restored to health and then together they launch out with another formation to catch up with the group.

Fit churches follow the pattern of geese but use some of the following ministry approaches to build a loving community.

Building a Loving Community

First, fit churches nurture an atmosphere of acceptance and love among their people. Walk into any church and you can sense the atmosphere. While it is hard to put a finger on what atmosphere actually is, it is easy to feel it, especially when you're a newcomer.

The sounds, smells, colors, lighting, and noisy buzz of people gathered in a close space create the atmosphere. It is especially noticeable in the welcome or lack of welcome newcomers receive, the willingness of people to talk to strangers, and the laughter that wafts over the conversations. The makeup of the worship team sends a strong signal of acceptance or rejection to people as they observe the ages, ethnicities, and personalities of those on stage.

Second, fit churches offer a small group ministry to build community. Developing a network of small groups within the church community is almost a necessity. People are looking for close, personal relationships. Intimacy is key, and for this reason, small groups are an extremely important aspect of church fitness. Small groups must be designed for a variety of needs: study, personal growth, ministry, worship, pastoral care, evangelism, and special needs or tasks. Nearly all fit churches have at least one support or recovery group. While a small group ministry does not guarantee a church will be fit, a church will be limited without it. Therefore, fit churches offer small group experiences built around people's needs. Typically, in fit churches, over two-thirds (70 percent) of the members attend a small group, and they talk positively about the level of spiritual care they receive.

Third, fit churches welcome and follow up with guests well. One of the most overlooked areas of church fitness is the process for making guests feel welcome and following up with them after the service. The church, more than any other organization, should be open to greeting and connecting with newcomers. Fit churches take full responsibility for incorporating guests into the community by designing an intentional flow of ministry that touches on the following six areas of ministry.

> *Connecting.* Helping new people understand and become a part of the church beyond Sunday morning worship.

> *Learning.* Helping people discover their unique talents, passions, and gifts.

Growing. Helping people grow spiritually as they use their gifts in service.

Matching. Helping people find appropriate places to serve inside or outside of the church.

Coaching. Helping people develop in their ministry experiences.

Recognizing. Helping people celebrate the way God has made them and used them in ministry.

Fourth, fit churches help people make friends in the congregation. Jesus said, "By this all men will know that you are My disciples, if you have love for one another" (John 13:35). People will drive a long way to connect with a church that provides substance beyond simple words such as "we care" and "we're glad you're here." While most churches are friendly, what most people want are friends. Thus, fit churches organize ways to help people build friendships. This may be done through programs (e.g., couples' fellowship dinners), creating centers for community (e.g., some churches rearrange church facilities to create several places for people to gather casually), or stressing involvement in small groups. But fit churches realize people must find at least seven friends in a church if they are to remain for a significant period of time.

Fifth, fit churches handle conflict well. The stresses and strains created by changes in a growing church quite regularly lead to conflict. In some cases, the conflict is simply between a few people, while in other cases it is church-wide. Yet fit churches have found effective ways to handle conflict in a responsible and biblical manner. In most situations, the church board has received some training in conflict resolution and is thus prepared for disagreements that may arise. Leaders deal quickly with issues rather than letting concerns reach a pressure point that may explode into larger conflict. People are urged not to listen to criticism but to encourage critics to speak directly to the individuals being criticized. The pastoral staff and visible leaders model healthy respect and support for one another, even when everyone does not agree. Leaders hold to the principle that "Those who know don't talk; those who are talking don't know."

Sixth, fit churches provide regular opportunities for fellowship and community. The early church devoted much energy to "fellowship," which was demonstrated in the fact that they regularly "were together" and took "their meals together" (Acts 2:44, 46). As a result, the believers "were of one heart and soul" (Acts 4:32). No doubt the busyness of our society makes it difficult for God's people to spend time together. Thus, fit churches provide multiple ways for people to gather in fellowship. Some churches provide low-cost meals so families can gather at church on a weeknight. Other churches schedule quarterly or monthly events to encourage people to come together in fellowship. A few churches with enough space have started food courts to encourage worshipers to stay around after the worship service and talk with others.

Five Types of Churches

Beginner Churches

Beginner churches welcome guests in a haphazard manner. Newcomers are left on their own to make friends and find a group or class in the church's ministry program. The atmosphere is usually friendly on the surface, but it is difficult to break through the social barriers to be accepted into the community. Long-term members sense the church is a loving community, but newcomers are not so sure. These churches offer a few classes or small groups, but they are often sealed off from newcomers due to the tight friendships among class or group members.

Plan of Action If You Lead a Beginner Church

- Analyze how many guests visit the church each year and how many stay for six months or longer.
- Organize a team to begin designing a welcome plan for newcomers.
- Encourage the pastor to preach or teach on the topic of welcoming strangers in the Bible, applying the theme specifically to the church.
- Interview a few new people to get their impressions of the church upon visiting.
- Seriously consider how the church can improve guests' first impressions.

Novice Churches

Novice churches have taken the first steps to becoming a loving community. At least one church-wide fellowship time is scheduled a year and everyone is encouraged to attend. These churches have established initial small group ministries and at least two small groups or classes are offered for every one hundred adults.

Plan of Action If You Lead a Novice Church

- Recruit some newer people (those who have been in your church less than two years) to oversee the church's welcome ministry.
- Conduct a focus group with some of the newer attendees to reveal the barriers to their involvement in the church community.
- Start or build on the church's small group ministry by adding some new groups so that at least three small groups exist for every one hundred adult attendees.
- Schedule at least two all-church gatherings per year to help build friendships and community.

- Have the church board or leaders complete a Bible study on how to handle conflict biblically.

Intermediate Churches

Intermediate churches have made a commitment to enlarge their small group ministries and are attempting to keep a ratio of four small groups for every one hundred adults in the church. Leaders have spoken to newcomers and have a good handle on the ways in which the church's atmosphere is both positive and negative, and they are attempting to create a more welcoming atmosphere. These churches recognize the importance of helping people make friends and build a sense of community and have started programs to improve in this area. They also offer at least two church-wide fellowship times each year.

PLAN OF ACTION IF YOU LEAD AN INTERMEDIATE CHURCH

- Have the church's connection team visit other churches to learn the best welcoming practices.
- Send the leader of the welcome team to a conference on connection ministry.
- Bring in a conflict management specialist to train church leaders on handling conflict well.
- Start enough small groups to maintain a ratio of five small groups for every one hundred adult attendees.
- Schedule three to four church-wide fellowship events for community building this next year.

Advanced Churches

Advanced churches work hard to create an atmosphere of acceptance among their people. Leaders set the standard and intentionally recruit additional leaders to reflect the wide range of people in the congregation. These churches also establish enough small groups each year to keep a ratio of five small groups for every one hundred adults in the congregation. They arrange the facility to provide centers of community throughout the building and grounds (e.g., coffee shop and tables, fellowship areas with couches and chairs, etc.) and offer at least four church-wide fellowship gatherings a year.

Plan of Action If You Lead an Advanced Church

- Bring in a church consultant to evaluate the church's connecting ministry.
- Appoint a single person to oversee the small group ministry.
- Appoint a single person to oversee the connecting ministry of the church.
- Consider how the church might remodel to encourage more community engagement among worship attendees.
- Evaluate the atmosphere (sounds, smells, colors, lighting, and feel) of the church and make corrections as needed to improve it.

Elite Churches

Elite churches maintain a practice of starting new small groups so about 20 percent of its total groups are less than two years old. A small group pastor oversees the entire program, and enough small groups are started to maintain a ratio of seven small groups for every one hundred adults in attendance. There is a well-planned and executed welcome and connecting plan in place for reaching new guests, which is evaluated and tweaked yearly. These churches also offer numerous fellowship gatherings throughout the year so everyone has the opportunity to meet others.

Plan of Action If You Lead an Elite Church

- Hire a full-time small group pastor.
- Hire a full-time connections pastor.
- Maintain a ratio of seven small groups for every one hundred adult attendees.
- Host a church-wide event on how to handle conflict in the church.
- Complete an entire evaluation of the church's connection ministries every three years and make ample adjustments as needed.

People will not stay long at a church if they do not feel accepted and embraced. In an increasingly disconnected world, the church that provides a means to assimilate people will heighten its loving community factor. People long to be part of an authentic community. Do all you can to meet this need.

Main Points

- *Beginner church*: friendly but not warm.
- *Novice church*: begins to intentionally develop an assimilation process.
- *Intermediate church*: regularly evaluates how people are assimilated.
- *Advanced church*: a variety of small groups and fellowship events cultivates a sense of community.
- *Elite church*: a key leader oversees the connecting of new people into the life of the church.

Vision-Directed Systems

Do you know Daniel Burnham? You most likely have never heard of him, unless you are an architect or a historian. He was a North American architect who designed the master plans for Chicago and downtown Washington, DC. He was also responsible for developing a number of buildings in New York City. No doubt, he had the most impact on the urban framework for North American cities, as he even influenced the designs of Cleveland and San Francisco too. Some feel he invented the profession of urban planning. Burnham even designed a few of the first skyscrapers in the world, and his construction of the 1893 World's Columbian Exposition in Chicago inspired the "City Beautiful Movement." He declared we should do the following:

> Make no little plans. They have no magic to stir men's blood and probably themselves will not be realized. Make big plans; aim high in hope and work, remembering that a noble, logical diagram once recorded will never die, but long after we are gone be a living thing, asserting itself with ever-growing insistency. Remember

that our sons and grandsons are going to do things that would stagger us. Let your watchword be order and your beacon beauty.[1]

Burnham's short statement, "Make no little plans," is a watchword for numerous leaders today. He understood vision drives all things. Church leaders often say things such as "We have a problem with giving" or "We have a problem with a lack of volunteers" or "We have a problem with outreach." While they are correct to identify these as surface issues, they are wrong on a deeper level. The foundational truth is, if a church has a problem with giving, volunteering, outreach, or a host of other issues, it has a vision problem.

All people are "eye-minded." That is, they think, imagine, and remember in terms of images. Throughout the biblical record, God communicated with his people visually. For some, such as Daniel, God communicated through prophetic visions of the future (see Dan. 2:19; 7:1; 8:1); while for others, such as Abram, God used a natural experience of looking at stars in the night sky to expand his outlook (see Gen. 15:5). In every case, vision emphasized a connection between the spiritual world and the earthly world. The communicated vision ordered both worlds in a compelling and specific way that connected God's plans for the future welfare of his people to the actual experience of his people, while appealing to them to respond with faith and action.

Vision is such a crucial dimension that the writer of Proverbs 29:18 asserts, "Where there is no vision, the people are unrestrained, but happy is he who keeps the law." This oft-quoted verse reminds us of two key points. First, without the direction vision provides, people are literally "out of control" (unrestrained). Second, happiness comes from God's Word. Essentially vision gives people the purpose (direction) needed for a happy life, and the vision must be connected to God's Word. Thus, fit churches have a biblically informed vision for the future that is communicated in a way that gives a sense of direction to the entire congregation.

You might be a fit church if . . .

- You have a written statement of purpose.
- You have a written statement of vision.
- You have written goals and plans for the future.
- You have identified your core values.
- You base program decisions on your plans.
- You organize the church's systems to support the vision.
- You regularly reference your vision in meetings, at lunches, and in private conversations.
- You are known for trusting God and stepping out in faith.

Write the Vision

The Old Testament book of Habakkuk reveals insight on vision and its importance in guiding God's people. Not much is known about the prophet Habakkuk, but he was a contemporary of Jeremiah and wrote before Israel was invaded by the Chaldeans. At that time, unrighteous judges ruled over the people of Israel. Habakkuk was concerned God did not appear to act to stop the miscarriages of justice taking place among the people. He learned, however, that God saw the fraud and iniquity of his people and discovered God had a plan for the future.

God spoke to Habakkuk as if he were a sentinel keeping an eye on a fortified city. Habakkuk most likely did not go and stand in a watchtower. Rather, he assumed an attitude of watchfulness—both spiritual and physical. "In this spirit of alertness the prophet was ready to receive by revelation the response of God. The answer was first to his own mind and heart, and then to his people."[2]

First, God told Habakkuk to "look among the nations! Observe! Be astonished! Wonder! Because I am doing something in your days—You would not believe if you were told" (Hab. 1:5). This is where vision comes into play. That is, by looking at what God is already doing in the world. What we are seeking is not *our* vision but *God's* vision for the future. Far from being inactive, God's Holy Spirit is already at work in the ministry area of a church. It is up to the leaders to find out what he is doing. In the case of Habakkuk, God was raising up the Chaldeans to bring discipline to the Israelites. Once Habakkuk looked seriously at the world scene, he could see God was already acting.

If you want to find God's vision for your church, you must look at the church's ministry area, which should be no more than about a twenty-mile drive from your church's campus.[3] What is God already doing in the community your church serves? Who is responsive to the gospel? Where are the open doors for ministry? Vision starts by observing what God is already doing around the town, city, or community in which the church is based. Church leaders normally find potential vision where people are experiencing transitions, trials, or troubles; these happenings are often open doors of ministry. How could your church serve people during these times? Observe how God is already working in your community. If thousands of children are playing soccer each weekend or attending computer classes or spending time on their electronic devices, ask how your church could use those activities to engage them for Christ. As church leaders closely observe the movement of the Holy Spirit in their church's community, a vision—God's vision—begins to develop.

Second, as with Habakkuk, the articulation of a specific vision begins with a single leader who spots opportunities before others do. Who allows the vision's amazing potential to capture their heart before it connects with others' hearts. Who speaks forth the vision before others give expression to it. In all the years of our combined ministry experience, we have never seen a group of leaders develop a vision. Boards, committees, and other organized groups of people do a helpful job debating, refining, and confirming a vision. But rarely, if ever, does a vision—certainly not a big vision—originate out of group processes. The process of group decision-making naturally leads to acceptance of the lowest common denominator. That is, to obtain group consensus, the group reduces an idea down to its minimal components. This is hardly action leading to *big* plans.

Third, God told Habakkuk to "record the vision and inscribe it on tablets" (Hab. 2:2). This old adage is true: Nothing happens until it is written down. Leaders may dream about the future, but it is just a daydream until it is written down somewhere. Some church leaders may say, "We don't have a vision statement, but we know what it is." If that is true, then they should be able to write it down. However, when they attempt to write down what is in their minds and hearts, they find it difficult to do so. Writing down a vision forces church leaders to express their ideas specifically. It makes them engage in clear language. And it encourages them to remove foggy concepts. Most leaders put more time and energy into planning a Christmas or Easter event than they do into planning the future of the church. When faced with determining what God wants them to accomplish in the church, they have a difficult time deciding. The process of writing helps church leaders bring clarity to God's vision for their church.

Fourth, God told Habakkuk to write the vision so "that the one who reads it may run" (v. 2). "The one reading it was to run to tell it forth, because it was such a message of joy to Israel, telling them of the ruin of their enemy and their own deliverance."[4] When God told Habakkuk to write the vision, he wanted the vision written using clear language and large, legible letters so the people could understand it. Then, after the people understood it, they participated in spreading the vision. This is still true today. A clear vision, clearly understood, leads to clear communication among the people and, we must add, clear acceptance of the future direction of the church.

Fifth, God told Habakkuk "the vision is yet for the appointed time; It hastens toward the goal and it will not fail. Though it tarries, wait for it; For it will certainly come, it will not delay" (v. 3). For Israel, this meant the people had to wait patiently for God's deliverance. God has an appointed time, and the vision cannot be hurried or delayed. It will take place in God's time. Church leaders find they want to hurry the fulfillment of the vision along, but vision is about the future—an appointed time. A church must long for, work for, and pray for it, while trusting in God to bring it about in his time. While we may think God is delaying, delay is just in the hearts and minds of people. Once the vision is written down and communicated clearly to the people, it hastes (as a rushing person panting for breath) toward completion. Vision seeks its own fulfillment and accomplishment.

Set the Pace

To return to our running analogy, among the crowds of long-distance runners are a few pacesetters. These people do exactly what the word implies—set the pace for the other runners. If someone did not take the lead and set the pace, the group would naturally slow down to the speed of the slowest runner (lowest common denominator). Records are never broken unless someone dares to move into the lead by setting a pace above what most of the runners would do on their own. The bottom line? Someone must set the pace!

This principle of pace setting is true in churches too. If a church wants to be above average, at least one person must jump into the lead and set the pace by communicating a compelling vision for its future. If you are that leader, consider asking the following.

Are We Afloat but Adrift?

People may not be able to state it, but most know when their church is afloat but adrift. They know when leaders are using problem-solving rather than strategic planning based on a big vision to guide the church. Problems, not a dream of what God desires, are setting the pace for the future. This attitude is revealed in statements we have heard in church conversations, such as "Our church is over managed and under led" or "We're making great time, but where are we going?" or "Our board takes forever to make a decision." Have you heard these or similar comments? If so, it is a somewhat silent plea for someone to set the pace.

Is Program #545 Really Needed?

Programs and church ministries are good and necessary in all churches. Any approach to reach, teach, or serve others must eventually be developed into an organized structure. Yet starting new programs may keep a church busy but become a substitute for developing a wider vision. The church ends up doing a number of good things but going nowhere. The best picture we can think of is that of a duck paddling furiously under the water but going nowhere above the water. Leaders must ask, "Is our 545th program going to help us become what God wants us to be?" Since programs are meant to meet a church's immediate needs, they often lack a sense of the eternal. Eventually people start wondering about the point to all the programming.

Am I Driven by CEO Matters?

Now by CEO we mean something entirely different from what may come immediately to mind. Church leaders, particularly pastors, are regularly "Consumed by Everyday Objectives" (CEO). The demands of sermon preparation, hospital visits, administrative details, constant meetings, pastoral care, and many other distractions hinder them from defining and articulating a big vision for the church. Of course, these routine objectives are good ones—even ones they must handle—but they do stop pastors from setting the pace with a full vision of the future. Some pastors are excellent at being consumed by objectives but fall short of their roles as leaders.

The problem for many leaders is their inability to find enough space in their busy schedules to even think about the bigger vision. Most pastors care about people and desire to be available to them. Being too accessible, however, can lead to problems in discovering God's vision for the church. In describing this issue, one pastor writes:

> Like most pastors, I enjoy being accessible. It makes me feel useful, almost indispensable. And after years of experience, I'm pretty good at overseeing the operations of the church. But there is a down side. Always being available drains me. When I'm drained, I lose perspective. I begin to think God's kingdom is our local church, and our church is one problem after another! Then vision is hard to come by.[5]

The fact is that being overly accessible may cause other leaders in a church to lose respect for the pastor. Why? Because they view him as not taking care of the important matters of leadership—articulating and communicating vision.

Can I Get Away?

It is normal for the immediate problems and objectives of ministry to take the time and energy of a pastor. The tyranny of the now has greater power than the future. Then too the problems of today are more pressing than the dreams of the future. As is popularly stated, "It is difficult to remember that your goal is to drain the swamp when the alligators are biting." If you want to dream a big dream, you must get away from the pressures of ministry and give yourself space to dream.

Gary remembers the difficulty of finding space to think and dream while pastoring a smaller church. To make room in his mind and heart to think about the future, he started going to the public library every Tuesday morning for about three hours. He would hide away in the back among some stacks of books to read and think. Only his wife and secretary knew where he was in case of emergencies. He also went once every quarter to a picnic area about thirty minutes into the mountains above the town where he lived. He took along his Bible, a notepad, and a sack lunch. This open environment gave him the space and freedom to think larger thoughts than he could experience sitting at his desk at the church. He discovered he was more creative in the mountains. His thoughts seemed to flow faster, and he regularly returned to church with a notepad of ideas and insights.

Whatever you do, you must find space to think and dream big. This means eliminating distractions and finding an environment that allows this to happen.

Our observations of pastors and other leaders who make the effort to get away to consider the future reveal a few things they do to make the most of their time.

First, take care of enough of the everyday issues and priorities so you can give your total attention to the future of the church.

Second, eliminate distractions, such as television, phone calls, and emails. How do you do this? Go to a place without television. Put your cell phone away for the day where you cannot hear it ring, beep, or vibrate. Leave your laptop on the desk at work. If you find it too stressful to be without your electronic devices, relieve the stress by calling home, say, only at 9:00 p.m. and just check emails once in the evening but never in the morning.

Third, take a Bible, notepad, and pens or pencils along but no other items that might distract you from thinking about the future. Most people find creative thinking happens better when they write or print by hand on a pad of paper than when they type into a computer. Besides, if the computer is around, you may be tempted to look at upcoming sermon notes or check emails or write a letter, all of which distract you from doing what you came to do—dream about the future.

Fourth, give yourself time to rest by just relaxing or, if you go on a retreat for a weekend, sleeping. The busyness of being consumed by objectives means we need time to de-stress. Allow yourself to do this without guilt. It is difficult to dream when your mind is exhausted. Then take time to read some passages in the Bible, asking God to convict you of any known sin. If you discover any specific issues, ask God for forgiveness. Clearing your mind and soul of clutter will open avenues for fresh thinking.

Fifth, ask yourself the following questions and jot down on your pad of paper the first thoughts that come to mind. Try not to polish or edit your thoughts or dwell too much on any one idea. The notion behind this exercise is to let your brain think freely while writing down everything that comes to mind.

- If the church I serve could be everything God wants it to be in five years, what would it look like?
- Where is God working right now in the church's ministry area, and how might we get on board with what he's doing?
- If I remain at this church another five (or ten?) years, what needs to change? What does God want to accomplish through me?

Sixth, allow your thoughts to settle for at least an hour or two, and then read over the ideas you've written down and organize them into categories or common themes. As you do this, begin writing a single sentence that captures the essence of what you are reading. In most situations, you will discover God gives you the words to combine your ideas into one complete thought. Feel free to rewrite this thought until it is compelling to you, capturing your heart, mind, and passion. This statement is or will become your vision.

Seventh, think of one real-life story that captures the essence of your vision statement. It is best if this story comes out of the history or recent experiences of your church. However, it must catch the attention of those who hear it and clearly illustrate your vision statement.

Eighth, resist the urge to preach about your vision or to speak about it to the church board as a group. Instead, if your church has less than two hundred members, speak to all of them about your vision before you speak about it publicly. If your church has more than two hundred members, you will not be able to talk to all of them individually, so make a list of the two hundred most-influential people in the church and then talk to them. As you speak to people, share the vision you discovered while away and ask, "If we were to go in this direction, how do you see yourself being a part of it?" This will reveal the extent of people's acceptance or resistance to your ideas. Listen carefully to any questions or objections, and begin to formulate answers or adaptations of the vision to address their issues. Always, *always* share the story that illustrates your vision, and ask them to pray with you as you formulate a fresh direction for the church.

Ninth, after (note: *after*) you speak to all the people on your list, then begin to preach and teach on the vision. By this time, you will have heard all the questions and concerns, making you able to speak to them. People will have prayed about your vision and discussed it with their social networks, so they will not be surprised when you speak about it publicly. Work with your church board to make the new vision a reality.

Tenth, begin to align all the ministries, programs, and decisions to the new vision. This is the hardest part of the process. You must execute the vision throughout the entire church, which will take time. At minimum, you must work to align the resources (money and people) to help fulfill the vision.[6]

Five Types of Churches

Beginner Churches

Beginner churches have no written vision statement. Leaders are concerned about immediate issues and needs and rarely give any thought to the church's future. They view the church as a ministry to maintain rather than a future to envision. Since no clear vision exists, the church's plans are limited to the immediate issues that arise. Essentially leaders are reactive rather than proactive in planning for more than a year.

Plan of Action If You Lead a Beginner Church

- Get savvy about vision by reading books and articles on the subject.
- Develop a vision for your own life before starting on one for your church.
- Ask God in prayer to reveal his vision for your church.
- Talk to other leaders about the future of your church.
- Request all leaders to report on the future of their ministries.

Novice Churches

Novice churches have started to discuss the conceptual need for developing a vision. Some form of vision statement is emerging out of the initial discussions, and church leaders talk about it from time to time when the idea arises. They have begun writing a strategic plan but have failed to execute anything they have come up with. The plan is a paper plan, not an action plan.

Plan of Action If You Lead a Novice Church

- Play catch-up by having a vision retreat with church leaders to develop a rough draft of your church's vision statement.
- Shop around to see how other churches are expressing their visions.
- Take five minutes of every meeting (formal or informal) to talk about your church's vision.

- As you go along, assess the needs you observe in the community and how your church might respond.
- Design a one-year plan built around your vision—and start executing it.

Intermediate Churches

Intermediate churches have developed a clear vision statement that has been published in several places—the weekly program, website, hanging banners, etc. At least once or twice a year the pastor spends an entire Sunday sermon explaining the vision to the gathered congregation. A strategic plan is in place, and it is executed intermittently.

PLAN OF ACTION IF YOU LEAD AN INTERMEDIATE CHURCH

- Refine your vision statement so it is clear and compelling. Use present tense and clear, concise language.
- Identify three stories that illustrate your church's vision and tell them over and over until people are tired of hearing them—then tell them some more.
- Chart your course by developing a strategic plan for the next two years.
- Forge a path to success by asking the pastor to reference your church's vision at least once a month in his preaching.
- Doggedly work at executing your vision.

Advanced Churches

Advanced churches have a robust vision, which everyone knows, believes, and can recite. Guests often hear people refer to the church's vision in conversations, and leaders make decisions with the vision in mind. A strategic plan is in place and executed almost 100 percent of the time.

Plan of Action If You Lead an Advanced Church

- Kick it up a notch by having the pastor refer to your church's vision every other week in their sermons.
- Get on track by writing a strategic plan for the next three to four years.
- Infuse your vision statement with passion and emotion by interviewing people your church has touched through ministry. Record the interviews and show them in a worship service and on your church's website.
- Paint a graphic verbal picture of the church God wants you to be in the next decade.
- Dream big—and focus on fruitfulness.

Elite Churches

Elite churches have a compelling vision. That is, people are captivated with the thought of helping fulfill it. People in the church are gripped with the church's vision and find it irresistible. They are drawn to give their treasure, time, and talents to empower its success.

Plan of Action If You Lead an Elite Church

- Host a vision retreat every five years with your church leaders to rethink and plan for the future.
- Project five to ten years in the future with your strategic plan.
- Require all ministry leaders to develop their own vision statement that supports the larger church's statement.
- Hire staff members who believe, embrace, and pursue the vision.
- Reference the church's vision in every sermon or Bible study.

Many churches have a dream, but few have a vision. A dream is about the horizon. A vision is about a particular point on the horizon. A dream is cloudy. A vision is clear. A dream inspires, but a vision is implemented. Turn your dreams into a vision. It will be the vision that will compel your church to act.

Main Points

- *Beginner church*: emphasizes maintaining the church.
- *Novice church*: develops future plans and acts on the plans.
- *Intermediate church*: has a clear vision of the church.
- *Advanced church*: bases strategic plans on the church's vision.
- *Elite church*: vision drives the church.

DIVINE EMPOWERMENT

One summer day when Gary was a youngster growing up in Colorado, he discovered the power of a small magnifying glass. While outside, he found that by focusing the sun's light through the magnifying glass he could intensify the light to the point that it would start small twigs and leaves on fire. Unfortunately, some wayward ants experienced the power of focused light too.

In a similar manner as focusing the sun's light through a magnifying glass, fit churches use focused prayer to experience God's divine empowerment. Divine empowerment for ministry happens as a church targets prayer toward growth barriers, difficult problems, and conflicts that threaten to undermine the unity of the congregation. While all churches no doubt pray to some degree, fit churches use a strategic prayer strategy that trains and empowers people of prayer.

> **You might be a fit church if . . .**
>
> - You have an organized pastor's prayer team.
> - You have a specialized group of intercessors.
> - You are experiencing 10–20 percent yearly growth.
> - You have prayer partners for every staff member.
> - You have an active twenty-four-hour prayer ministry.
> - You have three to four all-night prayer events each year.
> - You have a full-time pastor of prayer ministry.

Jesus's Ministry

It is an interesting bit of Bible trivia that the twelve disciples only asked Jesus to teach them one thing—to pray. Luke recorded, "It happened that while Jesus was praying in a certain place, after He had finished, one of His disciples said to Him, 'Lord, teach us to pray just as John also taught his disciples'" (Luke 11:1). They never asked him to teach them to preach or to plan or to do countless other things thought to be necessary for ministry.

The disciples asked about prayer because it was an integral part of Jesus's life. The Bible records more than twenty-five prayers in Jesus's ministry. Four occurred during his first two years of earthly ministry, five during the first half of his third year, three during the second half of his third year, and four during the last week of his life. And this does not even take into consideration his high priestly prayer, what we call the Lord's Prayer, or his prayer while on the cross among others. The closer Jesus came to his crucifixion, the more he prayed.

Luke records that Jesus's public ministry began in prayer after his baptism (see Luke 3:21–23), and he habitually slipped away throughout his time on earth to pray (see Luke 5:16). Jesus prayed intensely before making important decisions (see Luke 6:12).

And he gave thanks in prayer quite often (see Luke 9:16). In fact, Jesus's transfiguration took place while he was praying (see vv. 28–29), and he praised God spontaneously in prayer (see Luke 10:21). He also prayed at the Last Supper with the disciples (see Luke 22:17–19), for Peter (see v. 32), with the disciples on the road to Emmaus (see Luke 24:30–32), and at his ascension (see vv. 50–51). Jesus prayed in the morning, afternoon, evening, and late at night. He prayed before major decisions, when giving thanks for nourishment, and during crises. He prayed privately while alone in seclusion, with small groups of people, and publicly with many watching. Jesus gave us an example that divine empowerment comes through prayer.

Power in Ministry

Ray Ellis, a former denominational executive, tells the story of meeting a pastor from Korea in California. Ellis invited the pastor to go to lunch, thinking he could share some ideas to help him see his church grow back in Korea. Ellis tells the story this way:

> During our lunch conversation I asked [pastor] Kim how things were going at his church. He said that when he went to his church there were 175 in attendance. I said, "That's a nice size church." I asked how things were going at his church now. He said, "Before I flew to California we had over 8,000 in our multiple worship services." I forgot about my growth strategies and pulled out a pad and pen and asked "How did you experience such incredible growth in your church?"
>
> He said that when he arrived at [his] church he didn't know much about being a pastor so he invited people to come to church every morning to pray from 5:00–6:00 a.m. Eventually about 300 came to pray on their way to work. So, I wrote down "pray at church."
>
> Then he pulled out a church program and brochure that listed 1,000 home groups. He said, "We gather in homes for prayer

and Bible study and invite our friends and neighbors to pray and become followers of Jesus." [So] I wrote down, "pray in homes."

He said, "On Saturday night I go to my church study and pray all night long seeking God's anointing and blessing on Sunday's services." [So] I wrote down, "Pastor prays at church all night."

I asked what else [he did] for church growth. He answered, "That's it."[1]

That's it! While we are not suggesting fit churches pray in exactly the same manner as the Korean church in Ellis's story (there are cultural differences to take into consideration), praying at church, praying in homes, and having the pastor pray is a good start for any church that is serious about being fit.

Note how prayer and fruitfulness are tied together in Jesus's words to his disciples: "I chose you, and appointed you that you would go and bear fruit, and that your fruit would remain, so that whatever you ask of the Father in My name He may give to you" (John 15:16).

In the context of the Gospel of John, fruitfulness appears to mean new converts. For example, earlier in his Gospel, John told the story of Jesus with the woman of Samaria (see 4:1–38). After she left Jesus to go back to her village, the disciples came and started talking with him. As Jesus spoke, he saw that the Samaritan woman was making her way back with a large crowd from the village. Jesus pointed to the crowd and said, "Lift up your eyes and look on the fields, that they are white for harvest. Already he who reaps is receiving wages and is gathering *fruit* for life eternal" (vv. 35–36, emphasis added). The fruit Jesus referred to was the new converts who came through the witness of the Samaritan woman. This is very clear from the following verses, which report, "From that city many of the Samaritans believed in Him because of the word of the woman who testified" (v. 39; see also Matt. 9:35–38). Fit churches stress the ministry of prayer as the way to divine empowerment of ministry.

Church fitness does not come solely by human action. God spoke about the importance of the Holy Spirit's divine empowerment through the prophet Zechariah: "Not by might nor by power, but by My Spirit" (Zech. 4:6). God's Word was for Zerubbabel in reference to the rebuilding of the temple following the Babylon captivity. Tradition says Zerubbabel placed great confidence in his own abilities, so God intervened with a message. "Not by might," God told him. The word *might* (*hayil*) means "strength" and is regularly translated *power* or *ability*. It suggests that might comes from organizational strength. In this context, it has reference to methods or techniques. Thus, God was telling Zerubbabel the success of his ministry did not rest in organizational ability, specific methods, or creative techniques. "Nor by power," God continues. The word *power* (*koah*) refers to personal prowess or potency, which "includes the idea of an individual's strength of body, character, and personality."[2] "But by My Spirit," God concludes. The word *but* indicates a major contrast between Zerubbabel's organizational ability and his force of personality. God's work was going to be accomplished by a different means—the Holy Spirit. It is not that organization is not important, nor that personality is somehow to be avoided (which clearly cannot be done). Rather, it means fit churches carry out ministry in dependence on the work of the Holy Spirit.

Developing a Healthy Prayer Climate

Fit churches tend to practice a good mixture of the following approaches to produce a healthy prayer climate.

Corporate Intercession

Spiritual energy is derived from corporate intercession. While prayer has always played an essential role in church life and ministry, little training has been given to developing prayer strategies, particularly corporate intercession. Think about your church. You may have a plan for the next few years, but does it include a specific strategy for corporate prayer? If your church is like most, it does not have such a plan in place. Fit churches effectively gather larger groups of people to pray. Some churches designate one specific night of prayer per month when several groups gather to pray. Other churches schedule forty days and nights of fasting and prayer.

Planning for Prayer

Longtime church consultant R. Daniel Reeves expresses the need for prayer as follows.

> Churches arrange for people to take charge of many areas of church life, missions, Christian education, music, etc., but rarely is there someone whose primary task it is to ensure that the prayer life for the church is in order. Many times prayer is seen as an auxiliary, behind the scenes activity, and is not among the visible, articulated tasks and goals of the congregation.[3]

Fit churches are able to point to a specific plan they have put into action. Though beginner, novice, and intermediate churches overwhelmingly acknowledge the importance of such prayer, in too many situations it is not planned or practiced.

Prayer Training

Fit churches have an intentional plan for training and organizing both corporate and individual emphases on prayer. They make prayer training a line item in the church budget and regularly purchase materials, which they make available to encourage people to pray. Fit churches also schedule prayer training events at least quarterly to teach people how to pray, as well as to pray together.

Intercessory Prayer Team

Individuals with what some might call "the gift of intercession" are identified, organized, and assigned specific targets for focused prayer. "Whenever a congregation decides to shift the corporate focus away from themselves in order to reach the unchurched, spiritual warfare will occur."[4] The intercessory prayer team prays specifically to protect the church from spiritual attack and for the removal of barriers to the church's growth and vitality.

Pastor of Prayer Ministry

Fit churches assign an individual with the gift of intercession to organize a significant prayer ministry in the life of the church. The person may be paid or a volunteer, but either way they aim to involve as many members of the congregation as possible in the church's prayer ministry. The number of people praying each week or month determines the ministry's success.

Staff Prayer Partners

Each pastor and key staff members recruit a prayer team to pray for them and their ministry in the church. Pastors in larger churches will sometimes have as many as 120 people on a prayer team. Pastor Max Lucado recalls:

> I was so convicted about the importance of prayer partners that I asked God to grant me 120 members who would covenant to pray for me daily and pray with me fervently. Upon returning to the pulpit I announced my dream to the congregation. Within a month exactly 120 people had volunteered to form the team. We divided the volunteers into four groups and assigned each group one Sunday per month on which they would arrive early and pray for the congregation.[5]

Six months after establishing the prayer partners, Lucado's church had broken Sunday attendance twice, finished the year over budget, added three new staff members and three new elders, witnessed several significant physical healings among church members, and experienced increased unity.

Five Types of Churches

Beginner Churches

Beginner churches talk about prayer but do little to practice it. The churches may distribute lists of prayer requests for members to take home, but no one monitors the members to see if they are actually praying. A few people gather to pray but never more than 5–10 percent of the total church. Prayer in meetings is perfunctory, offered with little passion.

PLAN OF ACTION IF YOU LEAD A BEGINNER CHURCH

- Make a comprehensive study of prayer in the Bible.
- Encourage the pastor to preach or teach a series on key people who prayed effectively, such as Daniel, Hannah, and of course, Jesus.
- Ask the pastor to begin recruiting a prayer team of two to twenty-four people.
- Start committing the church's plans to the Lord.

Novice Churches

Novice churches have a basic prayer chain whereby they communicate prayer requests to a small group of people to pray. On some occasions, 10–20 percent of the church is gathered in prayer.

PLAN OF ACTION IF YOU LEAD A NOVICE CHURCH

- Ask the pastor to recruit a prayer team of twenty-five to forty-eight people.

- Organize a twenty-four-hour prayer time once during the year.
- Meet once a month as church leaders to pray at least one hour together.
- Start looking for gifted intercessors you can draw together into a prayer team.

Intermediate Churches

Intermediate churches routinely commit the church's plans to the Lord. Generally, around 20–30 percent of the total attendees participate in prayer either privately or corporately.

PLAN OF ACTION IF YOU LEAD AN INTERMEDIATE CHURCH

- Ask the pastor to recruit a prayer team of forty-nine to seventy-two people.
- Ask all pastoral staff to recruit a personal prayer team of at least two or three people.
- Organize a twenty-four-hour prayer time twice during the year.
- Meet at least twice a month as leaders to pray together.
- Regularly pray for God to bless other churches in your community.

Advanced Churches

Advanced churches routinely commit their plans to the Lord to align with his purposes. When the leaders and congregations of advanced churches believe the Holy Spirit is working, they obediently and sacrificially seek to follow his leading. Worshipers are regularly encouraged to get involved in corporate prayer opportunities, and between 30 and 40 percent of people participate.

PLAN OF ACTION IF YOU LEAD AN ADVANCED CHURCH

- Ask the pastor to recruit a prayer team of seventy-three to ninety-six people.
- Organize a twenty-four-hour prayer time three times during the year.
- Hold a prayer retreat to train people in ways to pray and to actually pray.
- Train people in spiritual disciplines, such as fasting, private prayer, etc.
- Regularly give God the credit for your church's blessings.

Elite Churches

Elite churches fervently pray for the Holy Spirit to draw lost people to Christ and regularly hear reports of people receiving Christ. They identify, organize, and give specific prayer requests to intercessors. Small groups and classes involve at least 50 percent of the entire congregation in some aspect of prayer.

PLAN OF ACTION IF YOU LEAD AN ELITE CHURCH

- Ask the pastor to recruit a prayer team of 97–120 people.
- Organize a twenty-four-hour prayer time four times during the year.
- Identify and organize a team of gifted intercessors who will commit to praying an hour a day for your church's ministry and for specific requests from the leaders.
- Appoint a person to oversee the development of your church's total prayer ministry.
- Fervently pray for God to bring lost people to your church.

Imagine what it would be like if your church doubled or tripled its focus on prayer. Imagine the impact such a focus might have on people inside and outside the church. Imagine the barriers that might be broken, the conflicts that could be resolved, or the morale that would increase. Divine empowerment through prayer is a key to making these things happen.

Main Points

- *Beginner church*: talks about prayer but seldom really prays.
- *Novice church*: prayer is contained to small segments of the church.
- *Intermediate church*: all church plans are committed to God through prayer.
- *Advanced church*: the congregation is regularly encouraged to engage in prayer. The pastor models prayer.
- *Elite church*: prayer is central to the church's ministry.

PART 5

BODY
COMPOSITION

To tell if you are overweight, you must take into consideration the amount of bone, muscle, and fat in your body's composition. A critical measure used by medical professionals is body mass index (BMI). Having a physical BMI higher than 24.9 is considered overweight. BMI is an approximate indicator—a rough guide. It does, however, give you an accurate assessment of your physical fitness.

In a similar manner, it is important that a church measure its fitness level or BMI.

TRACK PROGRESS

How fit is your church? By now, you have some idea of the fitness level of your church. However, knowing more specifics can help you clearly understand your situation, set realistic goals, and measure progress.

Ready to start a fitness program? Increasing church fitness requires three steps. First, determine how fit your church is currently. Second, set goals to improve. Third, track your progress. Get started measuring your church's current fitness level by using the progress chart below. Doing so will give you a more specific idea of your church's body mass index (BMI). Completing the chart yourself is a good beginning, but combining the perspectives of several people in your church to complete the chart will increase the overall validity of the findings.

Let's get started. Complete the progress chart by following the instructions below.

Read through each of the key indicators along the left side of the progress chart and put a check mark in one box to the left that is the closest to your church's current reality.

Key Indicators	Beginner	Novice	Intermediate	Advanced	Elite
Budget for outreach	☐ 0–1%	☐ 2–3%	☐ 4–5%	☐ 6–10%	☐ 11% or more
Annual community events	☐ 1–2	☐ 3–4	☐ 5–6	☐ 7–8	☐ 9 or more
People involved in outreach	☐ 0–4%	☐ 5%	☐ 10%	☐ 15%	☐ 20% or more
Weekly pastoral outreach	☐ Not engaged in the community	☐ 1–3 hours	☐ 4–6 hours	☐ 7–10 hours	☐ 11–15 hours
Evangelism training	☐ <10% of adults trained	☐ 11–19% of adults trained	☐ 20–29% of adults trained	☐ 30–49% of adults trained	☐ 50% or more of adults trained
Yearly evangelistic events	☐ 1 event	☐ 2 events	☐ 3 events	☐ 4 events	☐ 5+ events
Conversion growth rate	☐ 0% conversion growth	☐ 2–3% conversion growth	☐ 5% conversion growth	☐ 10% conversion growth	☐ 20% conversion growth
Church plants	☐ No daughter churches	☐ 1 daughter church	☐ 2 daughter churches	☐ 3 daughter churches	☐ 4+ daughter churches
Community-focused prayer	☐ All prayer inward-focused	☐ Worship service prayer once a month	☐ Pastoral prayer always includes community needs	☐ Public worship, leadership meetings, small groups include prayer for community needs	☐ Special prayer events are organized for community needs
Community service events	☐ None	☐ 1 per year	☐ 2 per year	☐ Quarterly	☐ 6 or more per year
Awareness of community needs	☐ Little if any concern	☐ Limited awareness	☐ Aware of 1 or 2 community needs	☐ Aware of most needs and has programs in place to meet them	☐ Highly engaged in the community and is known for being a need-meeting church

Category					
Community involvement by members	☐ Concerned with only church involvement	☐ Pastor is involved in community	☐ 20% of members have a ministry in the community	☐ 50% of members have a ministry in the community	☐ 60%+ of members have a ministry in the community
People with a personal ministry	☐ <20%	☐ 21–30%	☐ 31–40%	☐ 41–50%	☐ More than 50%
Person responsible for ministry recruitment	☐ The pastor is the primary recruiter	☐ The pastor and a small committee do the recruiting	☐ Ministry leaders recruit their own workers	☐ Ministry Involvement Team does the recruiting	☐ Full-time pastor of ministry is responsible for recruitment
Acceptance of new people in positions of service	☐ New people are not allowed to serve	☐ Some new people are allowed to serve if they are trusted	☐ New people are allowed to serve in a few low-level positions	☐ New people are quickly encouraged to serve	☐ New people find numerous places to serve
Percent of people trained to discover their spiritual gifts and ministry passions	☐ <10% of people have received training	☐ 25% of people have received training	☐ 50% of people have received training	☐ Two-thirds of people (66%) have received training	☐ 70% or more have received training
Stewardship training	☐ Offer no regular stewardship training	☐ Preach or teach on financial stewardship once a year	☐ Offer financial stewardship training at least twice a year	☐ Offer financial stewardship training 3–4 times a year	☐ Offer financial stewardship training five or more times a year
Financial accounting	☐ Faithful volunteer handles accounting	☐ Informed volunteer handles accounting	☐ Professional accountant voluntarily handles accounting	☐ Part-time professional accountant on staff	☐ Full-time professional accountant on staff
Cash reserve	☐ Less than two months of cash reserves	☐ Three months of cash reserves	☐ Four months of cash reserves	☐ Five months of cash reserves	☐ Six months or more of cash reserves
Financial trust	☐ People have little trust in leadership regarding financial affairs	☐ People have some trust in leadership regarding financial affairs	☐ People have good trust in leadership regarding financial affairs	☐ People have much trust in leadership regarding financial affairs	☐ People have great trust in leadership regarding financial affairs

Key Indicators	Beginner	Novice	Intermediate	Advanced	Elite
Church multiplication	Gives no money to church planting	Supports church planting only through missions giving	Designates 5% of budget for church planting	Has started one daughter church	Starts a daughter church every three years
Establishes a leadership culture	The church has no definition of a leader	Leaders are defined as people who hold a position in the church	Leaders are defined based on competency not just position	Leaders are recruited and trained in identified core competencies	Leaders are consistently developed
Creates a leadership pipeline	Pastor is the sole leader in the church	Leaders are the ones already in place	Begins to identify potential leaders in the congregation	Invites potential leaders to participate in a development process	Has a process to develop leaders who develop leaders
Leadership multiplied	Threatened by the idea of new leaders	Warms to the idea of multiplying more leaders	Catches vision for multiplying leaders; researches best approach	Begins a process for multiplying leaders	High value on multiplying leaders in the church
Sending leaders	Would never consider sending out leaders	Holds on to the leaders it has	Develops leaders—but for ministry in the church	Develops leaders primarily for the church—but releases a few	Places highest priority on sending out developed leaders
Evaluation	Does not evaluate worship services	Evaluates worship services once in a while	Evaluates worship services once a quarter	Evaluates worship services once a month	Evaluates worship services weekly
Planning	Plans worship services the same week	Begins planning worship services two weeks ahead of time	Begins planning worship services three months ahead of time	Begins planning worship services six months ahead of time	Begins planning worship services twelve months ahead of time
Team	Pastor alone plans worship service	Pastor and worship leader plan worship service	Worship team of three people plans worship service	Worship team of four to five people plans worship service	Worship team of six or more people plans worship service

Category					
Purpose	Has not discussed the purpose of worship in quite a while	Has studied the purpose of worship within the last few months	Has articulated a purpose for worship and tries to organize the service around it	Has a clear understanding of the purpose of worship and regularly focuses services on it	Focuses worship services on helping people humbly respect and actively serve God
Pastor as a disciple	Never been discipled	Recognizes need to be discipled	Personally involved in a disciple-making process	Disciples others	Multiplies disciples
Definition of a disciple	No definition of a disciple	Researches Scripture for definition of a disciple	Has a clear definition of a disciple	Has a discipleship process built around the definition	Consistently adjusts the disciple-making process to produce a defined disciple
Disciple-making strategy	No strategy in place	Primary strategy is the pulpit	Pastor disciples others	Leadership disciples others	Every area of the church multiplies disciples
Evaluation of disciple-making	No evaluation is done	Evaluation based on completing a program	Evaluation is built around doing, not being	Evaluation is based on transformation of character	Evaluation is based on the multiplication of more disciples
Leadership perspective	Downplays importance of leadership	Low regard for personal leadership capacity	Initiates a personal leadership development plan	Develops other leaders	Multiplies leaders who multiply leaders
Leadership responsibility	Pastor takes no responsibility for results	Pastor spiritualizes leadership results	Pastor is increasingly aware of the responsibility to lead	Pastor leads in partnership with God	Pastor takes responsibility to do what can be done, trusting God for the results

Key Indicators	Beginner	Novice	Intermediate	Advanced	Elite
5 types of church leading	☐ Determines level of dissatisfaction in the church	☐ Develops a plan to move church toward more missional activity	☐ Devises a system to show progress in missional activity	☐ Expands the vision of the church	☐ Pastor moves from CEO (Chief Executive Officer) to SEO (Spiritual Executive Officer)
Pastor's personal leadership development	☐ No personal development plan	☐ Attends one conference and reads one book per year	☐ Attends at least two training conferences and reads at least four books per year	☐ Has a full, written leadership development plan in place	☐ Presents a year-end report to board regarding progress on personal development
Connection ministry	☐ Has no formal welcoming ministry	☐ Has a welcome team but no clear plan or strategy	☐ Has a welcome team with a developed strategy, but it needs improvement	☐ Has a fairly good welcoming ministry, led by a volunteer team	☐ Has a well-designed and effective welcoming ministry
Number of small groups per attendee	☐ Has a ratio of 1:100 small groups (one small group to every 100 adults)	☐ Has a ratio of 2:100 small groups	☐ Has a ratio of 3 or 4:100 small groups	☐ Has a ratio of 5 or 6:100 small groups	☐ Has a ratio of 7:100 small groups
Handling conflict training	☐ Never talks about conflict	☐ Has discussed conflict at the board level	☐ Trains board and key leaders in conflict management	☐ Has held conflict management training for leadership	☐ Has held church-wide training on conflict management
Percent involved in small groups	☐ <10%	☐ 11–29%	☐ 30–49%	☐ 50–69%	☐ 70–80%
Vision	☐ Has no discernable vision	☐ Has an emerging vision	☐ Has a clear vision	☐ Has a robust vision	☐ Has a compelling vision
Strategic plan	☐ Has no strategic plan	☐ Has started to write a strategic plan	☐ Has a written strategic plan for the next two years	☐ Has a strategic plan for the next 3–4 years	☐ Has a strategic plan for 5+ years

	×5	×4	×3	×2	×1
Communication	☐ Never talks about vision	☐ Occasionally talks about vision	☐ Talks about vision once or twice a year	☐ Talks about vision consistently	☐ Talks about vision all the time
Execution	☐ Has no strategic plan to execute	☐ Has a strategic plan but fails to execute it	☐ Has a strategic plan and executes it intermittently	☐ Has a strategic plan and executes most of it	☐ Has a strategic plan and executes it completely
Participation in prayer	☐ <10% of people are involved in regular prayer	☐ 11–20% of people are involved in prayer	☐ 21–30% of people are involved in prayer	☐ 31–40% of people are involved in prayer	☐ >41% of people are involved in prayer
Plan for prayer	☐ Has no plans in place to increase prayer	☐ Has thought about some ways to improve prayer	☐ Has written down a few ideas to increase prayer	☐ Has started emphasizing prayer in most church ministries	☐ Has a well-defined plan for improving the prayer ministry
Prayer intercessors	☐ Has never discussed intercessors	☐ Has a few prayer warriors who pray	☐ Has identified some intercessors but has yet to organize them into a team	☐ Has an organized team of intercessors	☐ Has an organized team of intercessors who are actively praying
Prayer training	☐ Offers no training in prayer	☐ Pastor occasionally preaches on the importance of prayer	☐ Pastor preaches on prayer at least once a year	☐ Offers printed resources and classes on prayer	☐ Offers small groups or classes on prayer each quarter
Prayer events	☐ Offers no prayer events	☐ Gathers once a year for a special time of prayer	☐ Offers a prayer event twice a year	☐ Offers a prayer event at least three times a year	☐ Offers a prayer event four times a year
Total number of boxes checked in each column. Then multiply by indicated number.	_____ × 5 = _____ +	_____ × 4 = _____ +	_____ × 3 = _____ +	_____ × 2 = _____ +	_____ × 1 = _____ =

Add the total for the five columns together to determine your church's current BMI.

What is your church's BMI? The following scale is a useful guide.

Church's BMI	Fitness Level
50–100	Excellent
101–150	Good
151–200	Fair
201–250	Poor

Plan of Action

After tracking our progress for _____ (year), we find our church's BMI is _____ (insert number from progress chart). This BMI indicates we are likely a _____ (insert type of church).

To begin moving to the next level of fitness, we commit to the following fitness plan for the coming year.

Next-Step Action Plan:

Goal #1 (select one of the areas listed above from the left-hand column): _____

List three actions you can take to increase fitness in this area:

_____

_____

_____

When will you act on this goal? _____

_____

Who will hold you accountable? _____

_____

Goal #2 (select one of the areas listed above): _____

_____

List three actions you can take to increase fitness in this area:

_____

_____

_____

When will you act on this goal? _____

_____

Who will hold you accountable? _____

_____

Goal #3 (select one of the areas listed above): _____

_____

List three actions you can take to increase fitness in this area:

_____

_____

_____

When will you act on this goal? _____

_____

Who will hold you accountable? _____

_____

Epilogue

The Rest of the Story

Once Phil determined he needed to lose weight, he began his journey toward fitness with great enthusiasm. However, he soon discovered the initial enthusiasm wore off rather quickly. The motivation to start is good, but the discipline to continue is what really counts. Unfortunately, a large percentage of people who begin a fitness or weight-loss program tend to give up over the long haul. Research conducted by fitness experts shows only 5 percent of people who lose weight on a fitness or diet program keep it off long term. "They're the legendary 5% of people who have lost weight and actually kept it off for the long-term."[1] What it takes to lose weight or get fit is different from what it takes to keep the weight off or stay fit.

This is also true for churches. Church leaders get excited about helping their churches move toward fitness. However, most find starting easier than continuing on and finishing well. The pattern typically takes place just as it does with runners. Leaders start guiding their churches toward fitness with great enthusiasm. The initial positive outcomes are affirming, which empowers them for about a year. However, when they encounter resistance in the second year, their enthusiasm wanes. By the third year, church leaders give up.

Leading your church to a higher level of fitness takes determination and discipline. Here are five strategies to help your church be in the 5–20 percent who reach a higher level of fitness and . . . stay fit.

Keep fitness front and center. When a person begins moving from living an unhealthy lifestyle to a fit lifestyle, they may keep it quiet. The reason? They do not want to share their new goals with others in an effort to avoid being seen as a failure if they do not make it. Then if they do succeed, they can slack off a little bit without anyone knowing about it. Churches building the body keep the fit lifestyle before their people. The leadership publicly keeps all twelve of the characteristics of a fit church in front of their congregation by regularly reporting on the health and fitness level of the church. By doing this, leaders hold themselves accountable to work continuously toward a high level of fitness.

Devise an accountability system. Phil began his journey by tracking his weight every two weeks. He also kept records of distance and time for his running and walking. He made note of other workouts he did, such as using an elliptical machine or riding a bicycle. As a result, he could provide data on his exercise routine and any injuries that impacted his fitness plan. Keeping regular records allowed him to track his progress and be accountable. Churches building the body keep track of their progress. Your church will need a system to adhere to for accountability. A yearly report to your church or denominational leadership is fine, but it's best if you can keep a biweekly or monthly account of your progress. Using the three action goals from the last chapter, record a monthly account of your progress toward each one. Review them each month with your board, staff, or other key leaders.

Vary your workouts. The body is an incredibly adaptive machine. Doing the same workout for months results in the body adjusting itself and no longer gaining the long-term benefits of the exercise. This is why CrossFit programs are popular in running circles. CrossFit varies its workouts, including cardio, flexibility training, and weights. These variations result in continued fitness effectiveness. Churches building the body employ cross-fitness training, i.e., they must vary how they implement the twelve characteristics of a fit church. For example, while a fit church always needs to be evangelistic, how it implements evangelism must be varied or adjusted from time to time. The fact is that most church ministries tend to lose impact after they have been used for three to five years. Look over the twelve characteristics of a fit church and note how long it has been since each area has been revised. Any areas that have not been reworked in the last three to five years most likely have lost their impact. Pick one area and revamp it this year. Then retool another area the following year.

Keep a process perspective. Physical fitness is a process, not a point in time. It is not something you achieve and then neglect. It is continual, intensive, and intentional. It is a lifestyle. Churches committed to building the body see fitness as a process rather than an event. They understand fitness is a journey rather than a destination. Therefore, while church leaders begin with great enthusiasm, they realize it takes time. They are committed to the discipline of developing a lifestyle of fitness for the entire church. When you begin, be realistic about the future. Commit to the long term, realizing the first year will most likely be fun, but the hard work will come in the second year. However, if you stay with your program, you will find the best results in the third and fourth years.

Make setbacks stepping-stones. When Phil began his journey, he actually gained a pound by his first weigh-in. He was discouraged but not derailed. He continued working the plan and soon the weight began to come off. Injuries also occasionally limited his workout. One time he was diagnosed with a stress fracture in his left foot and was not able to run or walk outdoors, but he could work out on an elliptical machine or stationary bike. Although he could not do his regular workout, he did something to keep pursuing fitness. Churches building the body keep moving forward. There may be setbacks, but church leaders make them stepping-stones for future success. You may go through a season of frustration in one or more of the twelve characteristics of fitness but find other ways to accomplish them. Keep moving forward no matter how slow the progress. Leaders often overestimate what can be accomplished in one year but underestimate what can be accomplished in four to five years. Small steps of progress add up over time to equal big success.

The journey to becoming and maintaining a fit church is a lifelong pursuit. What it takes to get fit and what it takes to keep fit are two different processes. Each takes motivation, intentionality, accountability, and discipline. The church that embraces building the body engages the journey fully. May you be blessed in your pursuit.

Let's start building toward fitness today!

Acknowledgments

I want to thank my coauthor, Gary McIntosh, whose brief statement on "fit as opposed to healthy" was the seed planted that brought this book into being.

—Phil Stevenson

To our acquisitions editor Robert Hosack, our project editor Amy Ballor, and the rest of the excellent publishing staff at Baker Publishing Group. Your wonderful support, suburb editing, and ongoing encouragement helped make this book a better resource for every reader. We greatly appreciate all of you.

—Gary L. McIntosh

Notes

Introduction The Fitness Factor

1. "Ideal Body Weight for Men," Health Discovery, accessed May 16, 2017, www.healthdiscovery.net.

2. Bob Glover, Jack Shepherd, and Shelly-Lynn Florence Glover, *The Runner's Handbook: The Best-Selling Classic Fitness Guide for Beginner and Intermediate Runners* (New York: Penguin Books, 1996).

3. "Marathon Training Guide—Advanced 2," accessed April 5, 2017, http://www.halhigdon.com/training/51142/Marathon-Advanced-2-Training-Program.

4. John Bobalik, "How Are They Different? Elite Runners Are Born, Not Made," accessed April 5, 2017, http://www.active.com/articles/how-are-they-different-elite-runners-are-born-not-made.

5. Andrew Peloquin, "The 5 Components of Physical Fitness," FitDay, accessed May 17, 2017, http://www.fitday.com/fitness-articles/fitness/body-building/the-5-components-of-physical-fitness.html.

6. "What Is the Definition of Cardiovascular Endurance?" Quora, accessed May 16, 2017, www.quora.com/What-is-the-definition-of-cardiovascular-endurance.

7. "What Is the Definition of Muscular Strength?" Reference.com, accessed May 16, 2017, https://www.reference.com/science/definition-muscular-strength-c3cdc41064c118b3?aq=muscular+strength&go=cdpArticles.

8. Eric Brown, "What Is the Definition of Muscular Endurance?" Livestrong.com, January 27, 2014, www.livestrong.com/article/392246-what-is-the-definition-of-muscular-endurance/.

9. *The Free Dictionary*, s.v. body composition, accessed April 6, 2017, http://medical-dictionary.thefreedictionary.com/body+composition.

Chapter 1 Outreach

1. Gary McIntosh and R. Daniel Reeves, *Thriving Churches in the Twenty-First Century* (Grand Rapids: Kregel, 2006), 15.

2. Gene Wood, *Leading Turnaround Churches* (St. Charles, IL: Church Smart Resources, 2001), 151.

3. Ibid., 23.

4. George Barna, *Master Leaders* (Carol Stream, IL: Tyndale, 2009), 111.

5. Ed Stetzer and Mike Dodson, *Comeback Churches* (Nashville: B&H, 2007), 16.

6. Larry McKain, *Falling in Love with the Church* (Kansas City, MO: NCS Publishing, 2004), 103.

7. Larry Crabtree, *The Fly in the Ointment* (New York, NY: Church Publishing, 2008), 11.

8. Paul D. Borden, *Direct Hit* (Nashville: Abingdon Press, 2006), 66.

9. Reggie McNeal, *The Present Future* (San Francisco: Jossey-Bass, 2003), 25.

10. McNeal, *The Present Future*, 2.

Chapter 2 Effective Evangelism

1. "Lift," Aviation for Kids, accessed April 13, 2017, www.aviation-for-kids.com/Lift.html.

2. "How Airplanes Fly: A Physical Description of Lift," Aeronautics Learning Laboratory for Science Technology and Research (ALLSTAR), accessed May 16, 2017, http://www.allstar.fiu.edu/aero/airflylvl3.htm.

3. Dr. Rob Bell, "How a Mental Toughness Change Won Two Super Bowls," DrRobBell.com, accessed April 13, 2017, https://drrobbell.com/how-a-mental-toughness-change-won-two-super-bowls/.

4. James Clear, "Vince Lombardi on the Hidden Power of Mastering the Fundamentals," JamesClear.com, accessed, April 17, 2017, http://jamesclear.com/vince-lombardi-fundamentals.

5. Kevin Harney, *Organic Outreach for Ordinary People* (Grand Rapids: Zondervan, 2009), 62.

Chapter 3 Community Engagement

1. Milfred Minatrea, *Shaped by God's Heart* (San Francisco: Jossey-Bass, A Leadership Network Publication, 2004), 20.

2. Steve Sjogren and Rob Lewin, *Community of Kindness* (Ventura, CA: Regal Books, 2003), 20.

3. Hugh Halter and Matt Smay, *The Tangible Kingdom: Creating Incarnational Community* (San Francisco: Jossey-Bass, 2008), 124.

4. James Clear, "The Goldilocks Rule: How to Stay Motivated in Life and Business," *Huffington Post*, accessed April 13, 2017, http://www.huffingtonpost.com/entry/the-goldilocks-rule-how-t_b_10934176.

5. Hugh Halter and Matt Smay, *AND: The Gathered and Scattered Church* (Grand Rapids: Zondervan, 2010), 49.

6. George Hunter, *The Celtic Way of Evangelism* (Nashville: Abingdon Press, 2000), 19–20.

7. Ibid., 28.

8. Halter and Smay, *AND*, 54.

Chapter 5 God-Honoring Stewardship

1. Waldo J. Werning, "Managing Money for Christ's Kingdom," *Strategies for Today's Leader* 36 (Winter 1999): 4–5, 38.

Chapter 6 Leadership Development

1. John C. Maxwell, *Developing the Leaders Around You: How to Help Others Reach Their Full Potential* (Nashville: Thomas Nelson, 1995), 2.

2. Peter Economy, "44 Inspiring John C. Maxwell Quotes for Leadership Success," June 5, 2015, https://www.inc.com/magazine/201705/maria-aspan/flying-high.html.

3. Robert E. Logan and Sherilyn Carlton with Tara Miller, *Coaching 101: Discover the Power of Coaching* (St. Charles, IL: ChurchSmart Resources, 2003), 21.

4. Maxwell, *Developing the Leaders*, 3.

5. Kent Humphreys, *Shepherding Horses* (Oklahoma City: Lifestyle Impact Ministries, 2010).

Chapter 7 Christ-Exalting Worship

1. C. Kirk Hadaway, *Church Growth Principles: Separating Fact from Fiction* (Nashville: Baptist Sunday School Publishing Board, 1991), 62.

2. Dale E. Galloway, "Ten Characteristics of a Healthy Church," *Net Results* (May 1998):18.

3. James A. Stahr, "Christian Brethren Simplicity," *Christianity Today*, August 7, 1981, 21.

4. Robert E. Webber, "Church Buildings: Shapes of Worship," *Christianity Today*, August 7, 1981, 18.

5. Edward Sovik, "Planning for Worship" (unpublished paper, c. 1965).

6. Gordon MacDonald, "Three Elephants," *Leadership Journal* (Summer 2006): 108.

7. William Epley, "The Centrality of Worship" (lecture, Pastoral Ministry, Talbot School of Theology, La Mirada, CA, October 26, 2016).

8. Eddie Gibbs, *Body Building Exercises for the Local Church* (Falcon Books, 1979), 53.

Chapter 8 Disciple-Making Strategies

1. Aubrey Malphurs, *Strategic Disciple Making: A Practical Tool for Successful Ministry* (Grand Rapids: Baker Books, 2009), 19.

2. Leonard Sweet, *I Am a Follower: The Way, Truth, and Life of Following Jesus* (Nashville: Thomas Nelson, 2012), 14.

3. Craig Groeschel, Lecture at Catalyst Conference in Granite Bay, CA, 2012.

4. Mel Lawrenz, *Spiritual Influence: The Hidden Power Behind Leadership* (Grand Rapids: Zondervan, 2012), 56.

5. Malphurs, *Strategic Disciple Making*, 133.

6. Jim Putnam and Bobby Harrington, *DiscipleShift: Five Steps That Help Your Church to Make Disciples Who Make Disciples* (Grand Rapids: Zondervan, 2013), 41.

7. Malphurs, *Strategic Disciple Making*, 33.

8. Putnam and Harrington, *DiscipleShift*, 45.

9. Ibid., 51.

10. John Stott, *The Radical Disciple: Some Neglected Aspects of Our Calling* (Downers Grove, IL: InterVarsity, 2010), 135.

11. Robert E. Logan and Charles R. Ridley, *The Discipleship Difference: Making Disciples while Growing as Disciples* (Logan Leadership, 2015), 24.

12. Putnam and Harrington, *DiscipleShift*, 22.

Chapter 9 Pastoral Leadership

1. Lavern E. Brown, Gordon E. Penfold, and Gary J. Westra, *Pastor Unique: Becoming a Turnaround Leader* (Turnaround Pastors, Inc., 2015), 72.

2. James M. Kouzes and Barry Z. Posner, *The Truth about Leadership: The No-Fads, Heart-of-the-Matter Facts You Need to Know* (San Francisco: John Wiley & Sons Inc., 2010), 7.

3. Ibid., xv.

4. Todd Wilson and Dave Ferguson, *Becoming a Level Five Multiplying Church* (Exponential Resources, 2015), 99–100.

5. Jim Denison, "Gabby Douglas, Other Olympians Put God before Gold," Denison Forum on Truth and Culture, August 8, 2016, http://us1.campaign -archive1.com/?u=5369bb601ac44bfdda928110b&id=bc559114fd&e=e83f82 0791.

Chapter 10 Loving Community

1. Charles H. Kraft, *Christianity and Culture* (Maryknoll, NY: Orbis Books, 1979), 318.

Chapter 11 Vision-Directed Systems

1. Charles Moore, *Daniel H. Burnham, Architect, Planner of Cities* (Boston: Houghton Miflin, 1921), 147, archive.org/stream/daniel/burnhamar02 moor#page/n7/mode/1Up.

2. Charles Lee Feinberg, *Habakkuk, Zephaniah, Haggai, and Malachi: The Major Messages of the Minor Prophets* (New York: American Board of Missions to the Jews, 1951), 21–22.

3. Gary L. McIntosh, *Growing God's Church: How People Are Actually Coming to Faith Today* (Grand Rapids: Baker Books, 2016), 121–23.

4. Feinberg, *Habakkuk, Zephaniah*, 22.

5. Joel C. Hunter, "Clearing Your Vision," *Leadership Journal* (Spring 1991): 120.

6. For help writing a vision statement and strategic plan, see Gary L. McIntosh, *Here Today, There Tomorrow: Unleashing Your Church's Potential* (Indianapolis: Wesleyan Publishing House, 2010).

Chapter 12 Divine Empowerment

1. Ray W. Ellis, "Spiritual Factors Impacting Church Health and Growth in the 21st Century" (paper presented at the American Society for Church Growth, Golden Gate Theological Seminary, San Francisco, CA, November 12, 1998).

2. Richard Rigsby, "Not by Strategy, Not by Strength," *Talbot Times* 5, no. 9:3.

3. R. Daniel Reeves, *Preparing Congregations for the 21st Century: A Life Systems Approach to Strategic Planning* (Santa Maria, CA: Pacific Consultation and Mediation Services, 2000), 26.

4. Ibid., 27.

5. John Maxwell, *Partners in Prayer: Support and Strengthen Your Pastor and Church Leaders* (Nashville: Thomas Nelson, 1996), ix.

Epilogue The Rest of the Story

1. Mike Kramer, "5 Secrets of the 5 Percent," Spark People, accessed April 24, 2017, http://www.sparkpeople.com/resource/wellness_articles.asp?id=423.

Gary L. McIntosh is an internationally known author, speaker, and professor of Christian ministry and leadership at Talbot School of Theology, Biola University, in La Mirada, California. He has written extensively in the field of pastoral ministry, leadership, generational studies, and church growth.

Gary received a BA from Colorado Christian University in Biblical Studies, an MDiv in Pastoral Studies from Western Conservative Baptist Seminary, a DMin in Church Growth Studies from Fuller Theological Seminary, and a PhD in Intercultural Studies from Fuller Theological Seminary.

He is the author of twenty-five published books in the fields of pastoral ministry, church growth, and leadership, as well as hundreds of published articles in numerous magazines, newsletters, and journals. He is the bestselling author of *The Issachar Factor*, *Beyond the First Visit*, and *One Size Doesn't Fit All*. His most recent books include *There's Hope for Your Church*, *What Every Pastor Should Know*, and *Donald A. McGavran: A Biography of the Twentieth Century's Premier Missiologist*.

Gary and his wife, Carol, reside in Temecula, California, and have two grown children and seven grandchildren.

Phil Stevenson has an extensive background in coaching denominational leaders, pastors, and church planters. He has consulted on evangelism, church growth, and multiplication issues with a variety of denominations.

Dr. Stevenson currently serves as the District Superintendent of the Pacific Southwest District of the Wesleyan Church and is also a visiting professor at six universities and seminaries. He has a BA in psychology from San Diego State University, an MA in theology and philosophy from Point Loma Nazarene University (San Diego, California), and a DMin from Talbot School of Theology, Biola University (La Mirada, California).

Phil has published articles in a variety of publications and authored seven books, including *The Ripple Church*, *Becoming a Ripple Church*, *Five Things Anyone Can Do to Lead Effectively*, *Five Things Anyone Can Do to Help Their Church Grow*, *Five Things Anyone Can Do to Help Start a New Church*, and *The Leadership I*.

Previously, Phil served as the National Director of Evangelism and Church Planting for the Wesleyan Church in the USA and Director of Church Multiplication and Leadership Development for the Wesleyan Church of California.

He lives in Roseville, California, with Joni, his wife of over forty years. They have three adult children and seven grandchildren.

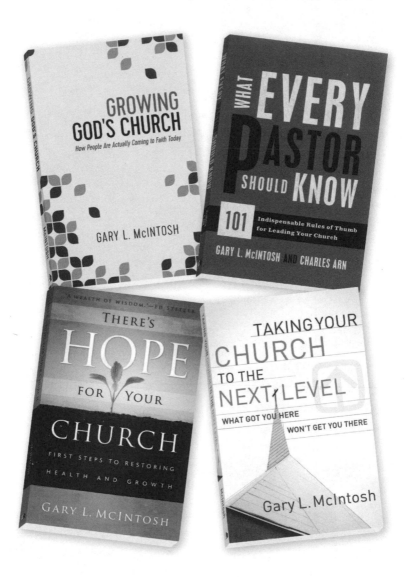